Teenagers
The Continuing
Challenge

Teenagers
The Continuing Challenge

SHIRLEY GOULD

E. P. DUTTON / NEW YORK

For Joe,
husband, lover,
partner, friend

Contents

Contents

Preface

When I was a little girl, it was the height of my ambition to be a good mother, knowledgeable in the ways of other human beings. My playmates thought about being teachers and nurses and secretaries and social workers, but I thought about motherhood. I didn't even play with dolls much, because for me they were poor substitutes for people.

Now I am a mother. The children I bore are now adult, independent, and launched in productive lives. We're friends. That makes me a successful mother.

Fulfillment of my ambition didn't come easily. The involuntary delay made the late blooming seem only richer.

Not for me the suffering, the whining, the complaining and the smothering so often associated with motherhood and ridiculed in the public eye. When my older two children were very small, I had the good fortune to be exposed to the teachings of the late Dr. Rudolf Dreikurs, who at that time led the Community Child Guidance Centers near my home in Evanston, Illinois. He taught me and then my husband to be effective parents. The education I got from him and his staff changed my life and the lives of those dear to me. Dr. Dreikurs not only taught me how to be a fulfilled woman, wife, and mother, but told me I am a writer and urged me to fulfill that role, too. Since his death I've devoted myself to that task, sharing with other parents the ideas and techniques I learned with his help.

In this book, I direct myself especially to those of you who are parents of persons between the ages of thirteen and nineteen, but everyone can learn something. The principles I shall discuss apply as well to any offspring for whom you have responsibility. If your children are not yet in their teens, you can prepare yourself. Meanwhile, study child guidance techniques readily available in the books of Dr. Dreikurs and many of his students (see Bibliography).

If your children are now past their teens, it's not too late to learn to be friends with them. You can't undo the mistakes you may have made, but you don't have to prolong them, either. It's not an easy task to revamp relationships based on decades of habit, but instead of thinking "The job is too big," try "Can I start with something small?"

Making peace between the generations *is* a tremendous task. It took us a half century or so to acknowledge that we were making war. We had to live through military wars and domestic upheavals while relationships changed. Blood was shed, shots were fired, and rebellions took place before we all became aware of the generation gap. Purely on a biological basis there will always be a generation gap; people have to reach a stage of biological growth before they can become parents. But we don't have to have psychological war across that generation gap.

You can make peace. I offer a whole platter of possibilities. You may nibble, you may snack, or you may devour the whole assortment.

Some of what I'm going to recommend may sound weird to you. You may become angry when you read my advice. The first time I received parenting advice I couldn't agree with was long ago, when my first baby, my daughter, was four months old. After her evening feeding, we would put her to bed for the night; an hour later she was up and crying, and the only way to quiet her cries was to bring her into the living room to be with us. When I asked the pediatrician what to do about it, he said, "Make sure she's all right, then turn out the light, shut the door, and pay no attention to the crying." All the way home from his office I fumed. As I pushed the buggy I thought, "He doesn't have to listen to her cry. How can he tell me to ignore her?" But I knew that I would have to try it, if only to prove that he was wrong. He was right. She cried for twenty minutes the first night, ten minutes the second, and the third night not at all.

I hope you will give my ideas consideration even if you don't agree at first. It gets easier and it gets better as you practice new ways. Join me. It's fun to be friends with your own children.

Teenagers
The Continuing Challenge

Introduction

When you become a parent for the first time, it's easy to suppose you're going to do everything "right." The newborn infant comes into the world seeming absolutely pure. That tiny person is in fact totally dependent on others to care for him or her, and the conscientious parent usually resolves not to make the mistakes that his or her parents made. A common resolve is, "I'm going to do things differently." When your children reach the teen years and you see how they have turned out, more often than not they are not what you expected and it's obvious that you can't do it over again.

Sometimes the dawning of the adolescent years brings a joyful surprise to parents, but usually there are pangs of disappointment. It's usually gratifying to marvel at the development of a young person as he or she stretches toward adult stature, but that pleasure is often dampened by the simultaneous realization that as a parent you can no longer have "control" over what that person does.

When a child is small, the control a parent can exercise is most evident because the child's world is limited. In the first year of life, the child cannot even move very far without the assistance of another person. Before school, children are mainly subject to the influences of their home and whatever playmates are available. Generally playmates are siblings, neighbors, or the children of parents' acquaintance. Children in the first few years of life have limited opportunities to widen their views.

Parents lose their ability to control a child's life as soon as that child leaves the home regularly, as in attending school, whether it be preschool, nursery school, kindergarten, or first grade that begins the school experience. Classmates, teachers, and casual acquaintances provide new references and perhaps new values. Children quickly learn that their choices are infinitely expanded in the world outside their homes. These influences increase in number as the years pass. And parents learn that only the control they have over their own lives, their own actions, remains constant. Even more startling is the realization that we never had complete control in the first place—only influence.

Control means power or authority. It means to direct or restrain and to regulate. True, we were able to control the surroundings and the situations, and we can always control our own actions and thoughts, but regardless of how it seems, each child is a self-powered individual who is free to choose his or her own behavior, thoughts, and feelings.

It may have seemed to you that you did have control over your young child. It may have been easy to regulate the activities, the waking hours, and much of the education of a child, but an adolescent presents a different set of realities. The natural development and striving toward adulthood that occurs in adolescence thrusts the young person toward a more independent identity that requires a move away from parental influence. Often it seems that he or she does so against the parents' wishes, but harmony between the young person and the parents makes this time easier for all. As in any other period of dramatic shifts in relationships, there will be some conflicting views and some upheaval, but there need not be continual chaos.

For a parent, one of the first requirements is some understanding of the adolescent viewpoint. All of us remember how we felt as teens, but the world has changed and continues to do so at such a rapid rate that our own memories may not be an accurate guide to the perception of our children's worlds.

One sensitive tenth grader expressed his own feelings in a poem:

Plea to Parents

Why do they do it?
What pleasure do they get by giving us hell?
Don't they understand what we are going through?
Were they somehow excluded from those years of turmoil
In the complicated cycle of life?
Why do they say "we understand"
When they don't?
Why
Do they ask us to talk to them?
Don't they realize the reason we won't
     is because we will
     be forever condemned
     for what we say in confidence and hope?
We need this time
     to search and explore
     to reason and find out
     to be or not to be.

We don't want to be told
>who our friends should or should not be
We want to decide for ourselves.
No
This is our time
Don't try to help
You must realize that we will rebel
>because each of us is an individual.
Don't tell us what to do
>Who to be
>How to behave
Let us be us
>and we shall find ourselves.*

To "find ourselves" adolescents must tackle and complete the following four tasks:
- Establish sexual resolution and direction
- Emancipate from parents
- Choose career goals and prepare for them
- Integrate personality

In earlier years, the child's direction was fairly well set by the parents. Parents choose the place a family will live, which in turn usually determines the school, the playmates, and the opportunities. The child has very little voice in the choices parents make about his or her environment, although, of course, the child's welfare may be prominent in their considerations. But as a child grows older and begins to separate from parents, he or she is faced with more and more independent decisions and greater responsibility for carrying them out. This in itself is a cause of friction between the generations. Parents are accused of treating their teens like

---

Personnel & Guidance Journal. vol. 52, no. 5, January 1974.

children, and in turn parents often accuse their teens of acting childish.

Variations of this dialogue occur often:

PARENT: You're old enough to take some responsibility
around here. Why didn't you wash the car?
SON: I was busy.
This is often followed by another interchange:
SON: May I have the car next week to go south during
vacation?
PARENT: No. You're not old enough to go alone.

It's no wonder that our offspring can't figure out where
they stand or when they're "old enough." A child may be old
enough to be a competent baby sitter but not old enough to
stay out after midnight; old enough to cut the grass but not
old enough to decide when it needs to be cut. Meanwhile,
parents continue to issue contradictory messages.

Preparation for decision-making ideally begins in the
cradle, where even an infant can choose to wake or sleep,
play or rest, coo or cry. As the child grows he or she can
choose what to wear, how and when to play, and whom and
what to play with. The child who has not been allowed to
make such decisions, who has not been held accountable for
responsibilities for his or her own life or the life of the family
will become the adolescent who resents dependence.

Many little children raise no objection to being ordered
around. They are obedient and seem to enjoy having their
parents, grandparents, and other adults tell them what to do,
when to do it, and how to go about doing it. These are the
children who get their senses of belonging, their feelings for
having a place in the family, of being accepted, from being
"good." Their parents bask in enjoyment of the obedient
child.

That child is, however, unprepared for the task of making independent decisions as he or she reaches adulthood. He or she is later likely to blame parents for not training him or her to choose, to decide, and to suffer the consequences of those decisions. That is the child who believes that a mistake must never be made, that a higher authority must decide the "right" thing to do and the "right" way to do it. He or she may become the adult who is easily manipulated by others.

In this case, the parents felt they were being good, generous, and kind to the child, but as the child reached the teen years, he or she may have responded by becoming mean, angry, and spiteful.

On the other hand, the child in another family, allowed to make personal decisions from the earliest age, will make mistakes because wisdom is limited and it is human to err. However, under the guidance of encouraging parents, he or she can be helped to learn from those mistakes. Furthermore, these parents would have exercised their influence by allowing the child choices in areas of minor importance, such as clothing choice, while reserving for themselves the decisions of greater importance, such as health and safety.

No child is to be allowed to decide when he or she can cross the street until he or she has been taught the fundamentals of careful observance and safety, nor until a parent has seen proof of appropriate caution. No young child is to be allowed to handle a lethal weapon, nor to make decisions about treating an illness or those involving the welfare of others. Parents must safeguard against danger. But the vast majority of daily choices can be made by the growing child so that his or her interaction with parents is a learning experience and a rich, affectionate relationship rather than a battle in the ongoing war between the generations.

When an adolescent appears to be making a mistake, he or

she must be allowed to experience the consequence of those actions. If an adolescent goofs off a whole term in school for lack of discipline needed to do the necessary work, the child should be allowed to fail. A parent should not pull strings or otherwise attempt to ensure a passing grade. Parents have been known to help with school assignments, write papers, and do research in order to guarantee success for their children. But the only guarantee such maneuvers yield is that the young person will learn how to manipulate adults. In no way can it prepare anyone for the responsibilities of living in the real world.

Even though mistakes have been made and initial damage has been done, the teen years are not too late to work on remedies. Once you, the parent, realize what has happened, search for the small ways in which a teen can be encouraged to make new decisions, encourage him or her to do so, emphasize your trust, and then move back. One of the ways the teen can make decisions is in apportioning the use of time; another is in choice of courses and extracurricular activities; surely another is in choice of personal appearance, clothing, and hairstyle. It is more important that the adolescent have confidence in his or her own decisions than that he or she conform to parental standards.

It isn't kind to abandon the teen who flounders, but neither is it helpful to continue protection. Life places demands on everyone, and each of us must learn to cope with those demands. Parents can't always be around to take away the hurt, nor can parents provide error-free lives for their children. Many parents believe that because they learned the "hard way" they can spare their offspring. On the other hand, don't we almost always learn from our own mistakes? Aren't our children likely to be able to learn from their own mistakes, too?

Emphasis on choice, on decision-making, is a reaction to

the idea that everything we are is predetermined. Psychology as expressed by many professionals has taught that we are a result of what we were born with and what our early experiences were. The individual's contribution to his or her own development was ignored and it was assumed that children could be shaped and molded to meet their parents' wishes. For almost a generation parents were advised by experts to love their children a lot, deny them nothing, and their psyches would develop straight and strong. Many parents feared setting limits because they might thwart their children's development. But an exaggerated permissiveness failed to produce the kind of young adults that most parents thought they were raising, and so the pendulum swung again.

Steadily, since Alfred Adler first published his ideas before 1900, his students have found that his basic theory of human personality continues to be applicable. It does not depend on the fad of the moment but helps people to reach their own potential and to be effective in their relations with others, especially in the relationships between parents and children. During his lifetime, the late Rudolf Dreikurs expanded Adler's theories into a practical system for parents which has been widely adopted and taught. It is described in his books *The Challenge of Parenthood* and *Children: The Challenge* and other books by his students, all of which are listed in the bibliography. In this book the advice is based on the work of Adler and Dreikurs.

Dreikurs's child-guidance techniques are most effective with young children. He realized their limitations when he excluded children over the age of eleven from consideration in the public family counseling sessions, which he recommended, and instead grouped them with their parents as near-adults. Thus, the older children were able to contribute to the solution of the family problems as adult peers.

Adlerian Psychology

Some of the basic tenets of Adlerian theory are that man is a holistic organism, a unified personality, always striving, always in movement. Adler was, and his followers are, optimistic about humanity's ability to cope with change. He saw people as mainly social beings, motivated by their interactions with other human beings. He coined the word *Gemeinschaftsgefuehl* to describe in German the concept of social feeling. He said that everyone needs to feel embedded in society, belonging to others with a feeling of solidarity. That word has been translated most often as social interest, and it also has been explained as humanistic identification. It connotes the ability to participate in and the willingness to contribute to society.

Adler's system is called individual psychology, derived from the Latin word *individuum,* which literally means undivided, indivisible, and refers to the unity of the personality. Adler's is a holistic system, referring to the whole rather than the parts, the unity rather than the fragments. Here we see the difference between Adler's position and that of Freud, who viewed the human being as a structure of id, ego, and superego. We who follow Adler see the person as a unified human being, functioning at all times as an organic whole.

It is a teleological system, emphasizing the goals toward which an individual moves rather than the circumstances that lead to the present state. Personality is not determined by outside forces but grows as the creation of the individual to meet his or her goals. Each individual behaves in such a way as to pursue personal aims, to meet unique purposes. In so doing, each person creates his or her own personality, that combination of traits, perceptions, and attitudes that forms an individual unlike any other, who struggles to attain distinct goals and gets into a neurotic bind if the destination is not reached. Whether or not the goal is attained, the individual continues to strive toward it, always retaining the possibility of changing or revising the goals and, subsequently, the techniques for reaching them.

Some of the goals common to many people are to be good, to be liked, to be first, to control, to suffer, to serve, to put others in our service, to create excitement, to get attention. We strive continually in the quest for significance, for a feeling of belonging. Just as living cells are in a state of continual growth and change, the human personality is in constant movement.

There is nothing inherently right or wrong about the goals a person chooses. In fact, they are usually not part of our conscious awareness but part of our general assumptions and perceptions. We shape our lives by how we pursue them. If we or our children pursue goals in constructive ways, we experience success and harmony with our fellows. If we choose instead negative, destructive ways, we experience chaos inside ourselves as well as in our relationships with others.

Adler's system is also phenomenonological in that it holds that people respond to life as *they* believe it to be, not necessarily to things as they are or appear to others. Each person—child and adult—has an individual perception of the world and the people within it. That perception is absolutely unique; no one else has that particular set of views and thoughts, and no one else can accurately know how it is and what it looks like. Another person can only guess.

Each person can only behave in the way that seems appropriate from his or her own viewpoint. People have choices and make choices but not in complete freedom. One can act only within the possibilities and within the situation he or she perceives.

One more attribute of Adlerian psychology is that it is an idiographic system. It says that each person, uniquely individual, has his or her own creativity, which is in use at all times. This means that personality is not molded in advance by heredity, nor absolutely controlled by environment, but that all the circumstances affecting the life of a human being are shaped by that person in the creation of his or her own personality. Adlerians do not put people in categories but attempt to understand each individual from the *individual's* own point of view.

The universal goal of all people is to be of value among other human beings. No one wants to be alone all the time; everyone craves satisfying relationships with others. The very survival of every person is dependent on interaction with others, from birth onward through life. That's the basis for the conflict between and among us. Everybody is constantly striving. Parents are striving for their own significance at the same time their children are striving to be independent. When the children reach the teen years and the normal course of life propels them to become more and more separate from their parents, the opportunity for warfare is there.

You don't have to read a book to know that parents and their children can make war. This book tells you how to make peace. We all have our ideas about how life should be. This book is about how life can be.

1
Why Is It So Difficult?

Why is it so difficult to get along with a teenager? You may be thinking that something is wrong with you because you find it hard, like Mrs. Collins, the mother of eight, who told me, "I really loved it when they were little. We would have had a dozen if I could have found some way to send them out of the house from age thirteen to seventeen."

Of course there are boarding schools for that purpose, but the vast majority of parents prefer to have their children with them. They want the continuity of family life, preferably without strain. Besides, boarding schools are very expensive and thus available only to the affluent.

Mrs. Collins was speaking of her first five children. There are three more not yet in their teens, and she is as eager to learn to live with them harmoniously as most parents.

The reasons for the difficulty fall into four main categories, which we will consider in this chapter.

The first problem is that *times have changed*. Times are always changing, but in the past several decades we have experienced a speeding up of the process, which often occurs so rapidly that we are hardly aware of what is happening. New technology in the form of transportation methods make distances seem shorter and faraway places closer. Progress has brought with it methods of communication that are immediate and profuse. Political developments have created revolution abroad and at home. Standards and values, religions and morals, have been questioned, and many accepted restrictions and limitations have fallen.

Another factor that contributes to the difficulty we have in getting along with our teens is that *our own expectations influence our relationships with our children*. Sometimes those are merely the ones we had for ourselves and never fulfilled. Often our children find them unacceptable. We expect their behavior and attitudes to meet our standards. We can't know our children's thoughts or feelings, and so we expect them to feel the way we did when we were their age. Or, what may be worse, we expect them to feel the way we *want* them to feel. Somehow, we parents get the idea that our children should function for our purposes rather than for their own.

Adolescence is a time of rapid and radical change in the physical anatomy. From puberty to maturity a child changes into an adult. The physical development follows a unique timetable, earlier in some and later in others. With the outward signs come internal changes. Not only do sexual stirrings occur along with the realization of possible adult sexual performance, but awareness of the necessity for planning to meet adult tasks of living also develops. New challenges arise in the teen years, and each child must find his or her own way to cope with them. Some meet those tasks and perform them successfully. Others avoid them. Still others will be shielded from making necessary decisions by well-meaning parents. No matter what happens during adolescence, at the conclusion of that period the person is a young adult. How successfully he or she will handle adult life depends largely on the kind of preparation that was available.

Finally *conflicting pressures* present a contradiction in norms for young people in today's society. The generally accepted value system stresses independence, autonomy, and individual freedom, while the ideal of a family is for its members all to be involved in a close relationship. The adolescent has to cope with that in addition to trying to find a way between doing what parents instruct in contrast to what one's peers are doing. All of us know the comfort of being in a group of people whose company we enjoy, who like to do the same things we do, who share our values and our hopes. It isn't hard to see that teens yearn for the same comfort; and sometimes the values of their friends conflict with the values of the family.

The Changing Times

Let's consider the first factor, the changing times. If you are now the parent of a teenager, you were probably born at the beginning of the second third of the twentieth century. Here or abroad, most homes at that time had electricity, a telephone, and a radio; fewer families owned automobiles, and hardly anyone had been in an airplane. Television was in the experimental stage, as were electric freezers, automatic washing machines, and air-conditioning. In your own youth, families generally stayed in one place. You were born where your parents lived and probably not too far away from where your grandparents and uncles and aunts and cousins lived as well. You even may have attended the same school your parents did and studied under some of the same teachers. Naturally, you can make up your own list of things we take for granted today that were not present in your own youth. Similarly, situations we took for granted at that time no longer exist today. Families have moved wherever opportunity directed, resulting in widespread dispersion. Moving the family used to be regarded as a major undertaking, but it is not anymore.

Even more important, in your youth, family life was stable. Divorce was a rarity, hushed up and excused. Even a broken engagement was a crisis. Most people expected to grow up, go to school, go to work, fall in love, marry, and live happily every after.

It may sound too obvious to call attention to the changes that have come about around us, but we must not ignore them. Our children are growing up in a world we didn't know. In fact, we find it very hard to make sense out of it for ourselves. For our children the perception is different. They were born into a world where mechanical and electronic inventions are taken for granted. In fact, it's a dull year when some new discovery doesn't capture the marketplace.

Our children don't have to put aside old ideas. They were born to new ones. Conflict arises only when we expect them to assume our ideas about how the world ought to be, and they see a world with different elements and different standards. They're forming their ideas, their views of the world, in an entirely different environment that deals with a reality different from the one we assume. Wanting to trust their parents' views, they can be torn between those standards and the lures of current culture.

The current culture offers an entirely new perception on life. Nancy Drew and the Hardy Boys are no longer the typical young people presented in literature, the movies, or on television. Education has changed and in some ways has brought a much broader perspective of life into the schools.

The old morality that prescribed standards for sex and sin no longer stands, and it is difficult for anyone to decide the limits of the new morality—if there are any. Standards in wearing apparel have changed so much that it seems anyone wears anything to go any place. Raw violence is with us in the living room daily, either on the news or on the television programs. Our national heroes are unfrocked in public and we wonder what has become of truth and honesty.

The most significant changes affecting all human relationships arise from the drives for equality among all oppressed people. In our own country we live daily with the changes brought about by Supreme Court decisions expanding the concept of equal rights for racial and other minorities. In this century we have seen the ranks of laboring people take on new dignity and seek a larger share of the production dollar. Not the least of the shoving aside of old notions comes from the realization by women that they too can be full participants in civilization. All of these changes affect our personal relationships.

Outside our borders, we see violent uprisings of ordinary people everywhere, wherever people feel they are living under injustice. Our official attempts to cope with such uprisings have not all met with success, and as individuals we are often bewildered by the outcome of government action.

You may be wondering what all this has to do with getting along with your children. You may think that your relationships with your offspring are separate from what goes on in the world, but if you do, you are in error.

Once upon a time the family unit could be self-sustaining, or nearly so. The family that lived on a diversified farm could grow its own food, spin and weave the cloth to sew its own clothes, find its own fuel, and create its own shelter. For tending to its physical ills, there were home remedies and medical doctors in the larger community who would come into the home to treat family members. (Remember house calls?) For tending to its communal and spiritual needs, there were churches and meeting places not too far away. News of the larger world traveled very slowly and could be thoroughly considered before it had any effect on the family unit. Life followed a predictable pattern, changing with the seasons, the rhythm of daily living following closely the rhythm of the sun and moon. Weather and daylight were the primary influences on the conduct of daily life.

Even in the cities, where the breadwinner left the home to earn money, the cooking was done at home and the family that ate together stayed together.

The advent of instant news made it impossible for anyone to be isolated from the rest of the world. Few of us would choose to go back to a time of household drudgery, of reading by kerosene lamp, of huddling around the stove to keep warm. The inventions of this century have brought us comfort, convenience, entertainment, and ease. But they have changed our lives in almost every aspect.

David and Vera Mace, marriage counselors and authors, have written:

> In the West . . . the process has now gone so far that it can hardly go any further. In the most progressive areas of the West today the wife's position is now so good that frequently she has more leisure, more power and more wealth than her husband. And we seem in some communities to be moving swiftly to the point at which children will have so much freedom that their parents will be powerless to exercise any great control over their behavior. Already some of the accepted behavior patterns, instead of being handed down from the previous genera-

tion as in the past, are beginning to be formulated empirically by the young people of the new generation.*

But that's only part of why it's so difficult.

Expectations

Our own expectations often interfere with our relationships with our children. Not only do we have expectations of what they ought to do and think and be, but we have expectations of ourselves, of how we ought to feel and behave as parents. We all want to be "better," whatever we want to be better than. It's true that growth is healthy, but ambition doesn't always lead to growth. Dr. Stern expects his son to want to be a physician and always has taken it for granted that he would educate himself to come into the practice. He is confused and crushed when Bob prefers to study music. Mrs. Duncan dropped out of college to marry and has been sorry ever since. She assumes Diane will welcome the opportunity to become an engineer, but Diane isn't interested in mathematics and would rather learn to cook and sew.

We remember our own teen years, not always with fondness, and want our children to excel in areas in which we were deficient. The madcaps who were always in trouble with the authorities hope their children will stick to the straight and narrow law-abiding path. The students who didn't pay enough attention in the classroom and thereby flunked their studies want their children to shine with knowledge. The wallflower hopes her daughter will be a big

*David and Vera Mace, *Marriage: East and West* (Garden City, N.Y.: Doubleday & Company, 1960), p. 279.

social success, even though her daughter would rather play softball. The person who was shy wants her child to be aggressive; the one who was aggressive wants his child to be less pushy.

In the competition for status, we don't always feel equal to the struggle, and so we look to our children to prove our worth. We really believe that we can act in such a way that our children will pile glory on our heads. That's great if they do, but if they don't, we feel somehow to blame. Sometimes, reflecting on our early years, we say, "After all, I didn't turn out so badly." We may be recalling severe punishment or gross indulgence, a protected, successful adolescence or a painful one. We seek justification for our behavior toward our own children so that whatever we do does not spoil their development. In our thoughts, we alter reality to suit our expectations.

There's a dreamy quality to a lot of this, as though wishing would make it so. It won't; the only way to help your child grow into a strong mature adult is to help him or her become independent of you. They must make their own mistakes and find their own wisdom. The greatest assistance you can give may at times seem like no help at all. Only if you keep in mind that you are striving to make and keep a friendship with a maturing individual can you find any lasting success.

There are two important rewards to be derived from following the system I recommend: one for the parents and the other for their children. Parents who allow and encourage independence have the freedom for life as individuals; their entire beings are not bound up in the parental role. Thus, when children do grow up and leave the family circle, such parents are not bereft. They may be lonely, but they are not suddenly robbed of the only role of their lives. They are able then to remain friends with their adult children while each generation pursues its own interests.

For the children the result is the self-confidence developed as a result of feeling independent, competent, and respected. Without self-confidence, no achievement brings joy. With it, one's efforts can be directed at productive work with resulting satisfaction.

And what of the success your adolescents would like to find? What are they up against as they move through the period of life between puberty and maturity? The questions stir inside them and we can't know what they are. Outward behavior gives clues, but the clues are not always reliable, and as parents we are often blind to their meaning. Parents are often amazed at the discoveries that emerge from their adolescents during family counseling. In my neutral presence many teens have found the courage to risk telling their parents, "I want to get even with you," or, "I feel worthless when you nag me," or, "No matter how hard I try, I don't feel as if I can please you."

Your expectations of your sons and daughters are one of the potent influences on their intellectual and emotional development. It can be profitable to examine them.

Physical Development

The third reason for difficulty among the generations is the inevitable and unpredictable physical development of the person in the teen years. Before this time, growth has been gradual, fairly regular, and almost predictable. With the onset of puberty, there may be a wild spurt of growth; the seedling becomes a tree. There is often an awkward weight gain. Even lack of growth can create a problem. The person who is the last to grow is acutely aware of his or her classmates' stretch.

Sexual development is simultaneous and presents a greater challenge. The girl whose bosom remains flat may feel at a disadvantage to the one whose bosom blossoms. And the buxom one feels proud and vulnerable simultaneously. The boy whose sexual organs grow large feels proud in the locker room, but this does not necessarily mean he feels proud of himself as a person.

There may be teasing by family and competition among friends that go along with the change in the shape of the body. Young people have no more control over others' reactions than they have over the growth of their own bodies, which used to be so familiar and suddenly have become so strange.

Nor do they have control over the sexual stirrings that become more and more insistent. The body demands, of both males and females, satisfaction of sexual desire, but the culture no longer gives clear and emphatic instruction. Not too long ago parents, schools, and religions were very specific about their instructions to abstain. Not everyone followed those instructions, but at least they knew what they were. There is some security in knowing what you're not supposed to do. You have a basis for decision, even if you decide to defy the rules.

With the relaxation of censorship, with freer living arrangements, with availability of automobiles, adolescents as well as adults are confronted with unlimited opportunities for freedom of sexual expression. These factors in themselves create difficulties, for each adolescent must make an individual decision of how he or she will cope with the very real sexual stirrings. In their relationships with parents, it has become increasingly hard for young people to know whether they are expected to do as adults do, as they say, as their peers dictate, or as the neighbors approve.

Conflicting Pressures

The fourth aspect relates to the difference in norms of behavior presented at home and outside, especially among peers. Each generation invents its own fashions in hair, face, clothing, hobbies, music, and other interests. An adolescent must taste many activities, many fashions, many ideas before he or she can make selections that will last. Adolescents must also test for themselves what they want in their own lives, what traits they admire in others, what principles they will uphold. There may be many changes in choice during adolescence, puzzling parents even more. They are expected to act like responsible adults. Until they can, however, they may skirt danger searching for excitement or for understanding. How can parents keep them safe? The brutal truth is that they cannot.

No parents can guarantee for a growing person that he or she will be safe, right, secure, and innocent through the parents' efforts. It was hardly ever possible. Each person must make his or her own mistakes and learn from them. When parents criticize or judge unfavorably they succeed only in widening the distance between themselves and their children. You don't have to approve, but you can refrain from comment. Parents must learn to distinguish between major and minor aspects of their offspring's lives in order to have as much influence as possible in major matters.

Further Problems

An expanding economy has made another opportunity available to many young people. In recent years it has become possible for ambitious youngsters to earn money beyond allowance funds, making possible the purchase of nonessentials: records, stereo equipment, automobiles, clothes. In many cases earning money, which grants a teenager a form of independence, has brought about greater division between parents and their offspring, often resulting, as well, in a physical separation at an early age. Further changes in the economic climate may make it harder for young people to earn money, but it is not likely to heal any rifts, nor to cause a return to the authoritarian families of earlier times.

One parent, troubled about the independence his daughter displays at age seventeen, asked me, "When is a child an adult?" There is no precise answer. An adolescent's life is fluid; he or she is neither child nor adult. As the adult aspect of the individual grows more dominant, the childish aspects still remain. One can have adult feelings and adult opportunities but is not an adult until he or she assumes adult responsibility for the total life.

What parents can do is think, understand, and work on the relationships between themselves and their children. The best opportunities occur when the children are young, when their home is the predominant influence on their lives. But even when they are young adults, it's never too late to repair a bruised relationship or improve a good one. Parents can help—but they can't control—the lives of their offspring. Parents can achieve happiness in their parenthood, but their children can't give them happiness. Much less is happiness available on demand.

What is available is harmony. In order to make harmony in music, you first have to learn the notes, then learn to sound them. Some notes may sound sour at first, but practice will ensure fewer of them as time goes on. As you read ahead, you will meet the notes and have the chance to create the harmony.

2
How Did They Get This Way?

In order to understand your adolescents and to learn ways to get along with them, it would be helpful for you to think about how they got to be the way they are. All of us have had life experiences that affect our current outlooks, and generally we assume our own outlooks to be universal. That is not so.

You are probably familiar with the term *lifestyle*. It has become part of the general vocabulary of newspapers, magazines, and electronic media. It usually means the style that people choose as their way of life, in the clothing they wear, the activities they pursue, the places they live and visit, and the values they adopt. In this book the term *lifestyle* means what Alfred Adler meant: the unified method of living a person adopts, incorporating that individual's perception of himself or herself, the surroundings and the universe, through which that person meets all of life's opportunities and challenges. Adler proposed that each person is a unity and thinks, believes, and acts always in conformity with the unified lifestyle developed at a very early age.

Rudolf Dreikurs, my own teacher, compared lifestyle to a musical theme that recurs continuously, bringing, in his own words, a "rhythm of recurrence into our lives."

Before adolescence, during the childhood years, your teen has tested perceptions and presumptions, confirming a unique viewpoint not only on the world, but on his or her own personal value, place in the family, and role in the school and community. Every experience a person has, from infancy on, becomes part of the substance that forms an individual's convictions. Each interaction with another human being is registered as if on an inner videotape, stored away to be retrieved by choice. Some recollections are kept available for ready reference; others may never be recalled again. One major difference between an adult and an adolescent is that the adult has had additional years of living experience during which he or she may have tempered the set of personal ideas and ways of relating to others.

Self-Image

In order for you to learn how to get along better with your adolescent son or daughter, or both, it is necessary to realize and accept that each of them is a separate person and their ideas about themselves and about life may be quite different from yours.

Ted Peterson, aged sixteen, looked handsome to me. He had attractive features, was tall and broad-shouldered with clear blue eyes and blond hair. But Ted didn't *feel* handsome. He wanted a smaller nose, longer fingers, and straighter hair. He didn't even like the color of his eyes—he thought they were too pale. His parents thought he was very bright and capable of doing much better work in school than his report cards showed. They would tell him constantly that if he would only study, he could be at the top of his class. They thought that was encouraging, but Ted felt that he couldn't make that peak no matter how hard he tried, so he didn't try very hard.

Ted felt he couldn't possibly live up to his parents' expectations of him, so, rather than study, he limited himself to the things he could do well: play baseball and build models. He and his parents needed to find ways to discuss their expectations. His parents especially had to understand that there is a great difference between how they regarded him and how he felt about himself.

Evelyn Grant was in a different situation. She was very pretty and she knew it. Her parents admired her and told her often how beautiful she was. But she was not flattered by their compliments, and they couldn't understand why. She felt that all that mattered to them was her beauty, for which she couldn't take credit. Her mother was a beautiful woman, too, and it was obvious that her good looks were hereditary. Evelyn craved comment about her achievements instead. She wanted to know that she herself was a worthy person, just as worthy as if she were homely. She was offended at her parents' praise for her physical appearance. It hadn't ever occurred to them that Evelyn felt unappreciated. When she was finally able to tell them how she felt, her anger diminished and their regard for her increased.

Highly intelligent people often hunger for compliments on their appearance, and sometimes beautiful ones prefer to be noticed for their brains. The young person who has limited assets profits from acknowledgment of any small achievement. You may not be able to tell how your offspring feels inside, and it is generally unwise for a parent to probe trying to find out. It is enough to observe and to realize that the inner perceptions and feelings may differ from what you would expect. If you crave communication from your teens, remember that it is far more productive to be available and to learn to listen carefully than to ask questions.

Personalities

You have probably already formed your own ideas about your teen's personality, possibly without being aware of the limits within which you view him or her. Labeling is dangerous precisely because of these limits, but we need to have some general shorthand way of describing combinations of traits. Among the ways teens may be viewed are these:

The victim. Whenever Jim gets any kind of an illness, he suffers. Even as a child, he'd run high fevers and have severe symptoms when other kids, exposed to the same sickness, had mild symptoms and recovered much more quickly. Things just seem to happen to him, and it's never his fault. His is the bike that gets stolen, his the jacket that gets torn, his the exam in school that was given without warning. The parent of such a person says, "I just wish I could help him more," or on the other hand, "I wish he'd take better care of himself and his things. Everything happens to him and he doesn't do anything about it."

The topper. Susan is always the best at anything she does. She gets the best grades, receives the most honors, wins the most elections, and has the most friends. She plays the piano superbly and sings the lead in the school shows. She may even be the prettiest girl in her circles. But her parent may say, "It's great when she's on top, but she's absolutely crushed when she isn't. I don't know why she feels she has to excel all the time."

The pleaser. Steve gets along with everyone, from the child next door to the aged shut-in. Everybody likes him. He collects a lot of compliments from adults because he's so likeable. What price does he pay for pleasing everyone? His parents may not know, or may not connect his moodiness, his timidity, or his occasional outbursts of anger with his determined effort to make everyone he meets like him and approve of him. Somehow he formed the notion early in life that he is acceptable only when he pleases.

The critic. Beverly has rigid standards of right and wrong and judges everyone by them. She needs to be right at any cost and feels virtuous when she suffers for her beliefs. She cannot tolerate uncertainty in herself or others, nor can she tolerate a challenge to her beliefs and criteria. Her significance rests on her understanding that it is necessary to be right and she knows what right is. She wants to have the correct answer and the moral superiority that goes with knowing best. One of her parents may have similar rigidities and take pride that they have been transmitted. At the same time, both parents may wish she would bend a little. She may be lonely and hurt, bewildered that friends do not seek her out.

The stoic. Jay covers his feelings so well that he assumes the demeanor of a stoic. He insists, "Everything's all right with me." On occasions for joy or even for sorrow, he acts indifferent. He believes that he will secure his place in the family and in the world by not showing love, hate, fear, or anger. Maybe he got this idea by hearing repeated admonishments such as "Big boys don't cry" or "That isn't the least bit funny," or he may have discovered that severe punishment will diminish if only he doesn't show his hurt. His parents may wonder why he's so hard to reach and why things seem to affect him so little. Maybe they have tried to penetrate his shell without success.

The fighter. Debby is against everything anyone else proposes. She has a keen mind and a working brain but uses it to support her opposition to the whole world. Her sense of personal significance rests on being different from everybody else, and she feels she must constantly prove it. It is important to distinguish between the fighter who is in temporary rebellion and the one whose approach to life is one of opposition, but the most important thing you can know about a fighter is that you will never win an argument with such a person. No amount of evidence will convince Debby, for her inner logic requires that she demonstrate opposition at every opportunity.

This is not an attempt to teach you in one easy chapter to analyze and interpret the lifestyle your youngster has developed. To do so takes more training than you can get just from reading. But what you can get is an understanding of the different ways people grow so that you will not expect others to act and react as you do.

Personality Development: The Family Constellation

Often parents say, "But my first two children are so different I can't understand it. They're only two years apart, and they were raised the same way by the same parents and exposed to all the same influences." Of course they're different. Each one has had to find his or her separate place in the family.

Furthermore, neither the parents, the home, nor the influences are the same for each child. Alice, the first born, comes to a childless couple and can receive their undivided attention after she arrives. Whether or not she receives it, there is no competition for her. There may be competition in the form of a pet, a career, or children from another marriage, but by definition she is the first born of this particular couple and will always have that relationship to them.

Two years later Ben arrives. His parents are two years older and have had the experience of raising their first child to the toddler stage. They have lived through night feeding, teething, weaning, walking, and first words and will not be unaffected by those experiences. When Ben perceives his family, it will include a sister who can do and be many things he cannot yet achieve.

If Alice finds her place in the family by being good, obedient, sweet, kind, and virtuous, Ben will have to exercise other traits. The chair of the "good child" is already taken, and Ben, therefore, may seek to occupy the chair of the "bad child."

One of the first human needs of infants is to establish a sense of belonging, a sense of having a place among the people who surround them, usually the family into which they are born. Physical needs must be taken care of for survival, but as these needs are met, infants develop an awareness of people about them and how they are treated. Even an infant decides how he or she will respond.

For example, Alice found that her needs were promptly cared for as soon as she made them known. She was a contented baby. She smiled a lot and played happily with her toys. Ben found that he had to cry a while before he would be taken care of, and so he cried more. The baby who is greeted with a smile and a pleasant voice will respond with a smile and a coo as soon as physical development permits. Each infant chooses from his or her own repertory of sounds, gestures, and movements those which bring the desired responses.

This pattern of behavior forms the basis for the creation of the lifestyle. Each of us needs a place in the family and in the larger world, and we want to feel accepted as a full member belonging to the other members. Each of us craves attention and recognition from other persons, for the human is a social being dependent on relationships with others for physical and emotional health.

Personality Variations

For everyone the ultimate goal is more important than the road traveled to reach it. That is the foundation for the perceived difference between the personalities of the first two children. Alice and Ben both seek and need a special niche in the family but they move toward it in differing ways.

There are many variations in the combinations of personality traits that a person acquires, but it is important to understand the internal decisions each one makes, without even knowing they are being made. We know when we are making conscious decisions about anything, but there is a level beneath awareness that is virtually automatic. Each of us screens out a myriad of options that are not in line with our own preferences. The choice of traits and roles is not completely free but is limited to the options that are available.

Choices are restricted by the circumstances of birth. For example, Ben in the family just mentioned may wish above all else to be the older sibling, but this choice is not available. There is no way he can arrange to be born sooner. What he can and may do is to overtake Alice by working harder, doing more, making greater achievements. He may during adolescence grow taller and bigger than his sister. This is something over which he does not have control, but it will nevertheless influence his view of himself and his relationship with his older sister.

Adler spoke of the pampered child and the neglected child as having developed specific personalities in response to certain kinds of treatment. Such children will have difficulties in adolescence related to their lifestyle.

THE PAMPERED CHILD

Charles was a pampered child. He never lacked for anything, for his parents were able and more than willing to gratify every wish. He did not learn to do anything for himself until long after he might have. His mother tied his shoes, his father combed his hair, and he enjoyed these attentions. He is accustomed to getting anything he wants, to having his own way, and to having other people serve him. Throughout school his teachers felt kindly toward him and always showed appreciation for any effort on his part to be independent. In adolescence he will be expected to show more independence, to make some of his own decisions, and to carry out plans without prodding, but he is unprepared. Having been accustomed to the service of others, he probably feels inadequate to cope with life as an adolescent and eventually as an adult. He may exhibit this in many ways. One method would be to withdraw as much as possible so that what he perceives as excessive demands would not be made on him. Another would be an active rebellion against his parents' and society's requirements. Having been accustomed to receiving whatever he wants, he may feel that he can take anything he wants, breaking the law freely.

Each individual is a unique combination, and so it is impossible to predict the way a pampered child will develop. What is certain is that a child so treated is not adequately prepared to meet life's demands and the necessities of social living.

THE NEGLECTED CHILD

Donna, by contrast, was a neglected child. Because of the circumstances into which she was born, she received very little loving attention. She has had to scramble for herself since an early age and believes that she will have to continue doing so. From her observations, it appears she has no worth in the eyes of others, since she does not get their care or consideration. She feels she does not deserve it. She never has been taught to be a cooperative member of a family and may not even have seen how a healthy family functions. She feels that what she does is of no importance and goes out of her way to behave in a distasteful or actually illegal manner. Girls who have been neglected often appear sexually precocious. In their quest for affectionate attention, they run from man to man in a promiscuous fashion. Donna will continue to **feel** neglected unless she can become part of a situation in which other persons care about her and show her that they do.

Such stereotypes are exaggerated, and it is dangerous to apply them generally. Charles and Donna are described only to illustrate extremes of personality development. The majority of adolescents will develop between those boundaries.

You may have found suggestions in the foregoing that seem to identify characteristics of your own adolescent. There are many more variations. In each person there is a framework of ideas, attitudes, and concepts that unite in a particular lifestyle and influence every thought, act, and feeling that that person has. The lifestyle is not predetermined or innate, but a complex of chosen traits. The choices are made beneath awareness. They are affected by changes in life's circumstances and are often changed in psychotherapy, but everyday living is shaped by the interaction and interconnection of the lifestyles of people who come in contact with one another.

What is different about adolescents is that new freedoms and new opportunities become open to them constantly and create new possibilities for disruption and dismay. But all of the events of life are treated by an individual in accordance with his or her previously constructed lifestyle.

When you understand how each person differs in the view of his or her own self, his or her own life, other people, and the world, you are on the way to knowing how to improve your own relationships with your offspring and with others.

3
The Limitations of Management

You've read this far, and now you may be thinking that all you have to do is understand your adolescent and everything will be all right. You may even be feeling cheated. I offered to help you achieve harmony, and all I've done is to show a way in which to see your teen in a different light.

You may be wondering whether the fact that you are a person in your own right is being ignored. Are you to exert all your efforts toward being a better parent? No, you're a person, too. You're a human entity, entitled to respect, consideration, and a life apart from yours as a parent. But this doesn't need to lead you into inevitable conflict.

It is very important to discover and recognize yourself, to make clear to yourself what you value and what you don't, what you want and what you crave, what is real and what is fantasy. As long as you keep on living by wishing, thinking how great life would be "if only" things were different, you are depriving yourself and your family of the opportunity to live a richer, freer, more harmonious life. To free yourself for accomplishment, you must first discover the limits of what you can't do and prepare to abandon the wishing what others would do.

Each of us has real limitations. We have already discussed the impossibility of compelling another person to do something he or she absolutely won't. Short of an attack on your very life, can anyone else force you to do something you absolutely decide not to do? Or, in the reverse, can anyone stop you from doing something you are determined to do?

Let us take some examples from everyday behavior. Suppose you're on a diet. Can anyone prevent you from eating forbidden fruit? Even in hospitals, patients have been known to work out methods of sneaking snacks.

What happens if you announce you're going to give up smoking? When another person reminds you of your promise, teases you, and attempts in any way to enforce your decision, does it help or hinder? For many people, this merely sets up a feeling of rebellion, a determination to do "what *I* want."

Or suppose you, an adult, are required by your mother to telephone her every day and keep her posted on your life and your family. Can she *make* you do it? Not if you decide, even subconsciously, not to. You may make the phone call, but if you don't want to, you can find a hundred ways to make it unsatisfying to her in order to prove it an unreasonable request. You may call at an inconvenient time; you may "forget" about it altogether, or you may turn the conversation into an argument. There is no way she can make her demand compel you to fulfill her wishes. It is true that people can impose unpleasant consequences upon you, but in the end, you make the choice between those consequences and your own actions.

Every hour of our lives we are subjected to commercial commands to buy products. Persuasive as they may be, we don't do every single thing we are exhorted to do by the salespeople of the media or the marketplace.

Each person has control of only one individual, and that is oneself. By trying to influence and manipulate others by our own behavior, we often lose the control of that most significant person who lives in our own bodies.

This is not to justify selfishness or self-centeredness but to illustrate the very real limitations of our own behavior. Only when we can realize the futility of many of our efforts can we become productive in the areas in which we have the greatest power. Any relationship between two persons or among a larger group such as a family can be improved when the emphasis shifts from "How can I make you change?" to "What can *I* do myself?"

Very often when parents remove themselves from the attempt to control their adolescents not only is there less friction but there is improvement in the productivity of their teens' lives.

Raising children is not a choice between authority and anarchy. We are often led to believe that unless parents rule in an autocracy, there is no order at all; there is just total permissiveness. Parents who have reared their children in an authoritarian manner, where the bosses tell the slaves what to do, when to do it, and how to do it, find out when adolescence arrives that they can no longer enforce their decrees as they used to. In the very normal part of growing up, more opportunities are available for children to experiment with different activities. The child who has been rebellious will welcome the chance to do things that cause even greater concern for their parents. Even the child who has been docile all along discovers a greater world as he or she reaches puberty. These teens may cling to the family circle in the belief that they must wait for the authorities to tell them how to proceed. Either extreme is damaging. In either case parents may feel they have failed.

Consider the plight of Mr. and Mrs. Long, who consulted me about their sixteen-year-old son, David. He is bright, articulate, and has many interests, but he has virtually no friends and no social life. His mother had adopted the habit of urging him to go to school parties, to join clubs, to work on making friendships. But the more she urged, the more David resisted. Life at home was a continuous series of arguments with mother and son challenging one another to verbal duels and father often called in as peacemaker, a job he really doesn't relish.

Mrs. Long explained that it was very important to her that her son does not repeat what she sees as her own mistakes. She never had much of a social life and now regrets it. Father reported a similar situation, and together they do no entertaining, have a limited circle, and generally have a restricted social life.

I pointed out that in some ways David is merely following their example; that for him it is quite normal to pursue his own interests, to stay alone and apart much of the time. At any rate, the arguments between mother and son were only creating misery for the whole family, and her attempt to spur her son to social activities was not fruitful. By recognizing the limits of her own ability, Mrs. Long was able to accept her son's determination to set his own patterns. Several weeks later, after the arguing stopped, she reported to me that her son was spending less and less time alone and more and more with his peers. Mrs. Long had become convinced that her efforts to move her son seemed like nagging to him. She took my advice and decided that his life was mainly his own business, not hers. The arguing stopped when she stopped pushing him to do what she wanted him to do and allowed him the freedom to choose his own activities. When he no longer felt he had to prove his independence, he was able to seek out friends and enjoy their company. He still spends a lot of his time alone, but it is no longer a source of friction between him and his parents.

This brings us to another area of disagreement between parents and their teens, and that is the parents' attempts to select their children's friends. In many ways, parents do this without conscious awareness. Parents decide where the family will live, what school the children will attend, where they will attend worship, and what activities they will participate in. Children can resist church and piano lessons, but they can't do much about the place they live and the school they attend. That is generally fixed and permanent, and the people the children associate with are largely determined by those two factors.

When adolescence arrives, the scope of geography is broadened. The high school generally includes students from a larger community than the elementary school or the junior high, and often for the first time students meet fellow students who have different backgrounds and different ideas from their own. Curiosity about those alternative patterns is a part of growing up to want to know more about these other ways, and this often results in friendships that parents consider alien and deem unsuitable.

As many parents have discovered, attempts to kill such friendships are not often successful. At a time when a teen feels the need to branch out, to broaden, it is useless to tell him or her that the choices are bad. Nor is it necessary to approve. Remember that you must keep your own values and make no threats or promises that you cannot enforce. You may find that your values differ in many respects from those held by your adolescents. This may be temporary, or it may become permanent. In either event, it is important that each of you respect the other's right to choose and decide. Coercion can't work in the abstract.

For example: Your son is interested in a girl of whom you do not approve. By this time he knows whether or not you feel kindly toward her. You can't stop him from being interested in her, but you can maintain your own dignity. You don't have to lend him your car to go to see her; you don't have to give him money to spend on her; you don't have to invite her to your home. This is not manipulation, nor is it coercion. It is merely recognizing your own limitations in managing your son's life and living according to your own values.

If any of this is done with anger, it cancels out any good effect. You may decide to welcome her and keep your opinions to yourself. But no matter how you decide to handle it, you must recognize your own limitations: that it is his friendship at stake; that he will decide whether or not he wants to pursue his interest. The other side of the relationship is that no matter how hard he tries, he can't convince you if you remain opposed.

Often, in trying to persuade one another we end in arguments in which neither side can give in. This is well known in the situation where a young man or a young woman deliberately pursues a relationship with a member of the other sex to whom his or her parents are opposed. The greater the feeling of rebellion, the more likely the young adult will move away from the parents' position. If, however, parents can respect the right of the young person to have different standards and different feelings, parents are free to maintain their own self-respect. When parents cease attempting to control their offsprings' lives completely, not only do parents increase their own self-respect but they make it more likely that their children will experience an increase in self-respect, self-esteem, and self-confidence. Parents don't have to like what their teens do and say, but they don't have to take responsibility for it either. Only when parents and their children can treat one another as separate human beings can the natural familial bonds of affection flourish. Only then can there be mutual respect and encouraging warmth.

Mrs. Tomaselli came to see me about her daughter Kim, aged fifteen, who was very depressed. Mrs. Tomaselli felt responsible for Kim's sadness but didn't know how to help her. The family had just returned to American suburban life after two years in another country where Mr. Tomaselli was sent by his employer. In the other culture, Kim was very popular as the only American. She had many friends there and was accustomed to leadership. On return to the old home, Kim found that she could not attain a position of importance. The friends she counted on had all formed into new groups and she felt like an outsider. She became moody and lazy and blamed her parents for the change in her life.

Mrs. Tomaselli accepted the blame. As long as she attempted to explain and cajole and reason with her daughter about the necessity for the move, and especially as long as she kept promising that things would soon get better, Kim retreated further into her isolation and emerged only to do battle over small disagreements. What started as small disagreements, however, often escalated into major battles, causing real distress to the girl and her parents.

When Mrs. Tomaselli learned that she alone was not responsible for Kim's feelings and that Kim was capable of doing something about her distress, she was able to accept her daughter as she was. She ceased to remind her to do her schoolwork; she ceased telling her what to do and when to do it, but remained friendly and did not argue. Kim's distress was real. Her mother could not argue her out of it. They were engaged in a classic power struggle. A power struggle is like a tug of war between two people. As soon as one person lets go of one end of the rope, the war is over. They had been fighting over who would win, and as a result, the war couldn't end. Only when Mrs. Tomaselli learned that she could let go of the rope without a loss of self-respect could she begin to relate to her daughter in a nonhostile way.

The continuous struggle had side effects. Even though Mrs. Tomaselli had argued and fought with Kim, she still felt guilty of causing her daughter's misery and looked for ways to make it up to her. She found it almost impossible to say No to her. Even without requests, she showered her daughter with gifts of clothing and jewelry, far out of proportion to what the family income would allow. Kim knew why she received these gifts, and told me, "All I have to do to get anything I want is to sulk for a while. Mother is afraid to deny me anything."

Kim even told me she wished it wasn't so easy to get presents from her mother. She knows her mother feels guilty, and she knows just how to act in order to get what she wants. But this brings her no triumph. There is no joy in winning, but Kim has not yet learned the art of cooperative behavior. Only if her mother refuses to be intimidated by her sadness will that mood become purposeless. Only when her time and her energies are not consumed in the war with her mother will she be able to devote that time and that energy to the pursuit of more appropriate goals.

Dr. Rudolf Dreikurs in his book *The Challenge of Parenthood** presented the goals of children's misbehavior. Since

---

*Rudolf Dreikurs, *The Challenge of Parenthood* (New York: Duell, Sloan and Pearce, 1948), p. 190.

their first publication, the goals have been misinterpreted in many ways, but their basic premise remains. It is, that in any conflict between parents and children, the behavior of the children can be seen to have a specific purpose, and the response of the parent can be tailored in line with that purpose.

As we pointed out in Chapter 2, since all behavior has a purpose, it can be seen that every individual acts in accordance with his or her lifestyle, with the purpose of reaching a particular goal that may not even be known to himself or herself; that is, he or she may not be aware of the purpose of his or her own behavior.

Briefly put, the purpose of adolescent behavior is in line with the four tasks of adolescence outlined in the introduction to this book. The adolescent is trying at all times to achieve independence from parents particularly, even though his or her behavior may appear to be enhancing the very dependence on parents. In such a situation, the adolescent is seeking the servitude of others in order to avoid the responsibility for his or her own life and future.

Parents can contribute most to the wholesome independence of their adolescents by refusing to become or to stay entangled in their routine decisions, by realizing their own limitations of effectiveness, and above all by remaining friendly while still allowing the distance that will give the adolescent the space to breathe and move and grow.

In order to change the relationship with your teens, you must learn to extricate yourself from their activities, but not estrange yourself from them as people. You must learn to respect and trust the teen and to respect and trust yourself.

In short, parents of teens have to learn to "hang in there" but not "hang on."

4
Trust and Respect: Make It Mutual

Do you love your son? Do you love your daughter?

How can you tell? There is no accurate way. The truth is that our feelings toward our children vary, just as do our feelings toward ourselves and toward other people.

Sometimes you are so suffused with tender warm regard that it's almost too much to bear. You overflow with affection and gifts of your time and your substance. This sounds lovely, but it is not always reciprocated or appreciated.

Then there are times when you feel so much dislike, anger, distrust, and even revulsion that it seems you can't stand it. Those feelings are communicated and rapidly returned.

Even when you are annoyed, angry, or sad about your children, you still love them but are often afraid to show that love. Awkward as it may be, the big kids need their parents' love too, expressed in appropriate ways. They don't want to be cuddled as if they were babies but they still crave acceptance. If they are to develop into emotionally healthy adults they need to know that their parents are with them even when they may disapprove. They want and need their parents' trust and their parents' respect.

To create an atmosphere of loving cooperation requires effort by members of both generations. Usually parents must demonstrate their willingness to make the necessary effort to overcome the reluctance of their offspring.

Family relationships are complicated in many ways. Especially as children reach adolescence and the natural strivings for independence, there are innumerable stresses on the bonds of love. Even when parents are annoyed, angry, or sad, the underlying love remains. It is never extinguished, any more than the memory of the hurt is extinguished. It is often difficult to be certain of the love of children for parents, but demanding proof will not make it evident.

Keeping in mind that you can control only yourself, it becomes possible to decide what kind of atmosphere you want to work toward in your family. Most of us crave harmony, but don't know how to go about getting it. We each feel that we need to have things go the way that seems right to us, and when they don't, we feel entitled to hostile anger.

We are inclined to set up ideals of family life and then feel disappointed or angry when those ideals are not reached. Too often parents decide what their children should do and how they should feel. What would be more productive is to say, "How can *I* contribute to a better atmosphere?" and then to do it. This may require different responses, fresh approaches from parents toward children. It will probably require a degree of restraint and a lot of trust, but respect is offered only when it is given.

Consider the adolescent who feels that he or she is constantly being directed by an authoritarian parent. He or she may even follow the directives, but with compliance comes a feeling of incompetence so that the teen cannot feel confident of his or her own ability to cope independently with the tasks of life. If like Kim in the preceding chapter, a teen can manipulate parents, she will have no respect for them. Adolescents will respect their parents if they are treated respectfully and will show their love for them if they feel safe in doing so.

In the teen years, the whole family situation is different. Parents feel the movement of time; the years of their omnipotence have ended and they approach middle age. They are aware that there is a time limit on their tenure and time is running out. Simultaneously, the adolescent is beginning his or her adult life, aware of the necessity to complete the break from parents and struggling to do so.

Parents Are Still Needed

In working toward creating harmony in your home, keep in mind that the adolescents, even as they rebel, want to feel that they can still turn to their parents for caring support. No matter how vigorous the arguments, no matter how demanding the movement away from parents, the basic bond that existed before is still present. At this period the burden of maintaining it may fall more heavily on the parents than on their offspring. Young people will struggle to display independence even while yearning for the parental connection.

Let me illustrate the permanence of the parent–child relationship. Cynthia was twenty-four, planning her wedding. She had left home after high school, graduated from college, and had been successfully supporting herself in her chosen career in a city that was a day's drive away from her family home. She was independent, self-sufficient, and enjoying her life. When she and her boy friend, whom she met in the new city, decided to marry, she relished the opportunity to plan her wedding her own way, in the city of her childhood.

As the deadline date approached, with all plans proceeding in an orderly fashion, her independence began to weigh heavily on her. She was getting tired at that point of making all the decisions and doing all the work, and she said to me, "At times like this I wish to could go home to mommy and curl up on her lap." She knew she couldn't, and wouldn't, but the yearning was there. It was a relief to be able to tell it to someone. She couldn't confide in her mother, for that would lessen her independence. Their relationship was good, but Cynthia wouldn't risk losing her independent status by acknowledging her need. She feared her mother might take advantage of the situation and take over.

Another kind of mother-daughter relationship was demonstrated when Ruth, aged twenty-one, was preparing for her wedding. She and her mother worked together in planning the arrangements. She told her mother, Mrs. Young, "I don't want to buy a wedding dress. I want to make my own gown, train, and veil. I've dreamed of it all my life." Her mother cautioned, "You can't possibly do all that while you're carrying a full load at the university, living so far from home. When would you find the time or the energy? No, you can't make your dress. Let's start looking in the bridal shops."

Ruth retorted, "I'm going to do it whether or not you think I should. I'd really like your help in choosing the fabric and pattern. Will you help me, or do I have to do it alone?"

In the face of such a firm statement, Mrs. Young was pleased to be asked for assistance and happily arranged to meet Ruth for the shopping she preferred. The gown and train were finished during vacation, in ample time for the wedding, with Mrs. Young's minor assistance on final details. Ruth consented to have the veil made by an outside specialist, and both mother and daughter were pleased with the total result.

The difference in the two mother-daughter relationships occurred as a result of contrasts in the patterns of interaction between the generations in the two families. While Cynthia felt she couldn't risk confiding in her mother, Ruth felt free to be open in her disagreement with her mother. The Youngs had learned to cooperate even when they did not agree.

Wanting Acceptance

Parents are often tested by their teens to see if they are still loved. A mother who sought my help told me how hard she tried to understand her son's difficulties:

> Ken and I were talking about that last night. He's just now at the point where he wants to and is trying very hard to separate himself completely. He hates whatever he sees as remaining dependence in him on us. Some of what he sees as our hanging on to him, we see differently.

Mrs. Lowell went on to say, "I would like to have a kind of relationship with each of the kids where they can discuss with me whatever they want to discuss without the feeling that I would be shocked or angry." Mrs. Lowell understands the difficulties of being a parent of teens since she has been through it several times and has made many errors. She's still learning about herself and about them, and possibly the most valuable lesson she learned is that she has to accept them as they are if she wishes to continue to share in their lives. When her son Ray, aged sixteen, was asked what advice he would give to parents about getting along with their adolescents, he responded, "If parents would just let their kids *be* rather than try to change them, they would probably get along a lot better." Asked to expand that comment, he said:

> When someone is trying to change me, I get a very revolutionary attitude toward it and I want to fight back. But I would say that parents should just let their children be, their teenagers—not leave them completely alone, offer advice and comfort when they can but not try to change them.

On the subject of conflict with his parents, he commented:

> What makes me not get along with my parents most is that I feel now that I'm not an adult but I'm trying to be one and when they keep reminding me that I'm a kid, it makes me feel bad. It makes me want to do something rash.

I asked Ray what his parents say that makes him feel that way, and he replied:

> Especially phrases like, "You're only seventeen." That just makes me angry. I would say if parents would let their kids be and not try to change them so much but just give them confidence and let them know that they love them and they'll help them out with whatever they need, but don't keep reminding them about being just a kid.

Ray's advice can be summarized succinctly: "Don't ever tell your children anything they already know." Actually, repetition and reminding often feel like nagging to the recipient. Younger children may simply cease listening, but teenagers may be moved to anger and then revenge. Each adolescent is acutely aware of being "only seventeen" or whatever the current age is, and it is demeaning to hear it repeated.

Young people are in an almost constant state of change. The best way to influence them is to accept them as they are and let them know that you care about them as individuals. Ray says it clearly when he says "let their kids be."

Encouragement

Ray also offered a precise prescription for encouragement—the kind of encouragement that would help him feel more self-confident and less hostile. His advice goes like this:

> I come home with an idea that I really think is great, something I'm really proud of; when I tell it to my parents, *the only thing they need to do to make me feel good is to say "mmhm, that's great."* And stop at that. But when they criticize it and tear it down right in front of me, I walk out of there feeling awful. This separates me from my parents because then I end up not telling them about my problems or my feelings. I usually tell someone else instead, which just takes us further apart.

This sounded like a typical exercise of misguided parental wisdom. Many parents feel it is their responsibility to criticize, to judge, to inform their offspring from the heights of their superior knowledge, but what happens more often is that the younger person is discouraged and stifled in the expression of his or her ideas. Criticism ought to take a very minor role in family relationships—there's hardly any time when it is appropriate, and most of the time it's damaging.

Criticism implies fault-finding, and there's very little to be gained in family relationships by censure. You may think of a bit of constructive criticism, but remember that it is very unlikely that your adolescent son or daughter will regard any criticism at all as constructive. Suppose that idea is not what you consider good? Suppose you think it's awful? If you say so, you will do what the Lowells do to Ray: push him down. If you refrain from expressing your opinion of the idea, you place the responsibility for it where it belongs: on the person who conceived it.

Maybe you think you are giving constructive, helpful criticism. But fragile ideas need building up if they are to develop. Tearing them down with criticism, no matter how you think you're justified, only makes it more difficult for the teen to create new ideas and to trust your judgment. On the contrary, when you listen carefully and refrain from disparaging comment, you are treating your teen with respect and helping to create the kind of atmosphere that nourishes love.

Encouragement is elusive, but we all need it. It is easier to say what it is not than what it is. It is not lavish praise, nor is it continual reminders. A very discouraging remark such as "I know you can do better" is changed into an encouraging remark when it is phrased, "I know you can do it." It is not encouraging to say, "If you would only try harder," but it is encouraging to say, "Do you want to try it?" None of these phrases will be encouraging if they are said in an angry or impatient tone, but if the atmosphere is one of trust and respect, the effect can be to instill confidence—the courage to be and to do.

Don't Spoil the Triumph

Josh gave me another example of the destructive nature of criticism when he told me how his parents responded to his pleasure at being selected to be a speaker at high school graduation. He hoped his parents would be pleased and support his efforts. He tried to share with them his ideas for the speech and hoped they would like them, but this is the result he reported to me:

> I came home and told my mother about the meeting we had with Mr. Block when we decided what topic each of us would talk about. I told my mother what my topic was and what I would say about it, and she said, "Be careful." I said, "What do you mean by that?" She said, "Don't make it sound like you're talking about the whole school in general rather than yourself. I think you're taking on sort of an egotistic attitude."

Josh told me:

> That kind of tore my whole thing down. It didn't sound that way to me, and Mr. Block, the faculty sponsor, teaches speech, and he didn't think it came across that way either. It made me want to talk nasty to her, to say, "What do *you* know?" But I didn't. He's the speech teacher; he ought to know what's good and what isn't. He said it's good, so why not let it be good!

This was his interpretation of his mother's mild remark:

> It made me have echoes in the back of my mind like she was saying, "Don't venture too far, you're still a kid." "Don't try to be too much on your own." That's the thing that makes me angry the most—when I keep getting reminded that I'm still a kid and I'm trying not to think of myself as one.

Josh's mother took the joy out of his achievement when she attempted to be helpful. She damaged his sense of competence by disapproving of his ideas. She may have been trying to protect him, but she might better have accomplished her purpose if she said, "That sounds like a good topic. Will Mr. Block help you develop it?" or simply, "What an honor! It makes me feel good to think you're going to speak at graduation." If she followed with "Do you want me to help you with the speech?" Josh might have refused her offer, and she would have to accept his decision.

Consider that the speech at graduation would be made only one time and promptly forgotten, but the critical remarks are often habitual and result in feelings of inadequacy that may carry throughout life. If Josh's mother were less critical, the whole family could share his triumph with less emphasis on the speech itself.

What to Do

Find every way you can to show evidence that you have respect for your son or daughter as a person. Trust as much as you can, even when you feel that your adolescent has not been trustworthy. Think about the incidents in your own family that have turned out in ways that made you unhappy, and recall what you did or said in connection with those incidents. For no matter what the situation is, it can be exacerbated or alleviated depending on the response and reaction of family members. Perhaps you recall the time your teen was picked up by the police for speeding in the family car after curfew hour. Did you as a parent make it worse by the additional punishment you ordered and the harsh words you uttered? In the height of your anger, did you recall all the ways in which your teen had previously disobeyed and all the hurt you suffered? Did you say something like, "You're no good," thus opening the way for the young person to feel that "as long as I'm no good anyway, I might as well do what I want." The old saying "If you have the name, you may as well have the game" expresses a state of mind common to many discouraged persons. If you can't think of precise ways, use the general ones: refrain from criticism; accept the teen as a person of value; commend what is commendable and ignore what is annoying.

A Word about Love

Whatever love is, it does not blossom and flourish just because it has begun. In every human relationship, it needs continual nurture to stay alive and bear the fruit that is its reward. Between parent and adolescent, it is especially difficult to maintain the bond of affection while the young person is tearing away the bond of dependence. It is as though while the teen is moving onward, the parent must stay constant, growing as a person but not moving away from the position of care.

There will certainly be times when a parent will feel "She doesn't care a hoot about me," especially when the teen has defied a parental rule, but the action can be regarded in other ways, too. Each parent chooses the way to respond. If you choose to regard each defiance as an attack upon your love, you will be kept quite busy defending yourself. If you can accept your offspring as a separate human being whom you love, you will be more able to avoid the feeling of being personally beaten. Thus you will be in a better position to assist your child in making his or her way as an adult.

5
Communication

There are two basic varieties of communication: open and hidden. It's a difficult topic to consider, because in the very act of considering it we're doing it. There is probably some kind of communication among all the living creatures of the earth, but as human beings we are dependent on communication with one another for our very existence. It's easier to recognize open communication than it is to become aware of the hidden kind, but in order to understand our relationships with each other, it is necessary to consider both.

Open communication occurs when a spoken message is sent by one person and received by another. It is what the whole current science of communication is based upon: a message sent by a source, through a transmitter, accepted by a receiver, on its way to its destination. This broad general definition covers all the myriad sounds we are subjected to, emitted by human beings or by machines, some of which are transmitters for the human voice, others of which transmit sounds made by mechanical or instrumental means.

Hidden communication is all the other messages we send

to one another, mostly without being aware that we do so. It occurs in the form of body language, in what a person does as well as what he or she says. To understand it, one must watch the way someone moves rather than just pay attention to the sounds of that person's voice.

Is there more transmission than reception at your house? Are more messages being sent than are being received?

This is a complicated way of asking whether you, the parent, listen and pay attention to the many messages that are in the air around you. *Communication* has become a cliché word for most of us. We have become aware of its importance in our lives, and the lack of it has been offered as the reason for every marital conflict and many human difficulties. But the word itself has many meanings and many uses. It is important to understand at least some of the meanings in order to get a better grip on the possibilities for better relationships among family members.

Open Communication

First, think of the spoken messages you deliver and the way you deliver them. Pay attention to the sound of your voice, because everyone else does. You may think you are "asking nicely" when in fact the tone of your voice is commanding or nagging or downright insulting. Think about how you speak to friends or to people whom you want to impress. Do you speak that way to family members, and if not, why not? If your objective is to improve relationships with your children, it is very helpful to speak to them in the tones you usually reserve for the other people in your life.

It's amazing what voice inflection can do to the meaning of a statement. While it isn't possible to transfer the nuance of sound to the words in print, consider the difference in the following statements. In each one the parent was trying to encourage a son or daughter to make a personal decision:

"If that's what you think you really should do, go ahead, but don't come to me later if it doesn't work."

"Well, go ahead and do it if you want to."

"Why do you want to do that?"

"That's a good idea, but have you considered all the other possibilities?"

None of those statements indicates respect for the idea presented or encouragement. Each one tosses back a doubt, an antagonism. They all sound like *"Yes, but . . ."* as the speaker seeks to assert his or her superiority. Contrast them with a simple statement such as *"That sounds good."*

If it doesn't sound good to you, don't say so, but you can respond with a noncommittal "That's interesting."

To make it short is to make it effective. That statement does not grant a rubber stamp of approval but merely an assent that allows the listener to maintain self-respect and to develop more confidence in himself or herself and in the idea.

Too often parents spoil their opportunities for friendship with their children by belittling them every time they have a chance. Some parents may do this with the mistaken idea that it will help a young person to want to overcome feelings of incompetence. Others may do it with the mistaken intention of keeping their offspring dependent. Whatever the intention, parents may have many ways of reminding their teens that they're not grown up yet. Adolescents are very sensitive to such reminders. In the teen years especially, it is important to allow young people space and time for the development of new ideas. Both parents should be aware that their adolescents need to experience a broadening of their own abilities to make decisions. If parents wish to continue to be consulted occasionally, they must be careful not to put their teens down, not to squelch their ideas, not to engage in verbal karate. A parent may win the argument but lose the confidence of the young person. An empty victory if there ever was one.

In learning to keep your mouth shut, it is helpful to consider the purpose of your remarks. Very often, a person thinks, "It just came out of me" or "I didn't mean to say it; it just erupted." While this may seem to be the case, the underlying reason for caustic comments is related to a person's general goals. A parent, especially, may be trying to prove he's right, or she's the boss, or they know best. A more constructive goal is to improve the relationship.

When you are trying to learn to control your verbal criticisms, examine your own motives and values. Which is more important, to be able to say "I told you so" or to have a harmonious bond with someone? Generally, an improvement in the relationship will remove the necessity for anyone to prove who's right or who's boss.

The objective is two-way communication, not a one-sided harangue or a retreat into cold silence. The climate to aim for is the one in which people can speak their thoughts and their ideas to one another in a helpful manner. Keep your mouth shut while you listen, and continue to keep it shut until you have formulated something to say that does not demean another person. This does not mean that a parent must agree with everything a teen says or give that teen everything he or she wants. The most effective system is to decide what you yourself can do and stay within your own limits.

Mrs. Mitchell reported an interchange with her fourteen-year-old daughter. Some time before at a family meeting it had been decided that Jane would not leave the house after 8:00 P.M. on week nights. One evening Jane announced that she was going to the library and moved toward the closet to get her jacket. The following conversation took place:

MRS. M: Are you going out? You agreed that you wouldn't.

JANE: But it's so boring around here. There's nothing to do here, and the kids will all be at the library.

MRS. M: This is a school night, and I thought it had been agreed that you'd stay in.

JANE: I know, but I want to go.

MRS. M: I can't stop you, but I don't like it. It makes me feel that the decisions we make together don't count.

JANE: They do, but I do want to go.

MRS. M: I'd rather you didn't.

The tone of Mrs. Mitchell's voice remained conversational. She stayed in her seat and did nothing to try to stop her daughter except to tell her of their prior agreement. She realized that she could not restrict her except by force, which was, of course, out of the question, and she was more interested in remaining friendly and treating her daughter as a separate individual over whom her control was limited. After this interchange, the daughter moved back into the living room and said no more about going out. A harmonious relationship had been established, and Jane didn't want to disrupt it completely either.

In discussing the two basic varieties of communication, open and hidden, I have emphasized open communication because it is more available to description in print. In order to understand hidden communication fully, moving pictures would be more appropriate.

In addition to what you say, another important but often overlooked aspect of open communication is how you say it, and how you address the person to whom you speak. Do both parents call each other by name, or do they avoid using their given names in talking to or calling one another? This in itself results in a depersonalization and shows a lack of respect for the humanness of the other individual.

In an earlier time, I recall a storekeeper who summoned his wife from their living quarters in the rear with, "Oh, dear," when he needed her help. Of a conservative generation, he hesitated to use her given name in front of strangers. But today it is more likely that a man belittles his wife by calling her "the little woman" behind her back or "mama" in her presence. She may retaliate by calling him "boss" or "daddy," and they may both call their children "hey." The message here is this: Use the name by which your teens wish to be called, and use it with respect.

In working for better communication, you must also learn to listen. You must train yourself to listen intently and accurately, not just to hear. While you listen, you must keep your mouth shut. So much of what passes for conversation in families consists of persons talking *at* one another rather than *to* each other. It is as though each person is following his or her own script, hardly listening to the other except for the cue word which makes it possible to come back with the next line. If you don't believe it, make a tape recording of any family conversation at your house. Let the tape recorder run for a half hour of ordinary family interchange, and listen to it later. You will probably hear one of two basic versions: One person dominates while another tries to be heard and the others who were present will hardly be audible; or two persons will constantly be competing to dominate the conversation.

If you find some conversation boring, examine the underlying reasons. Are you bored with the subject matter, or are you using boredom to relieve yourself of the responsibility of paying appropriate attention to another person?

Often boredom is a selfish excuse to retreat from interaction with other people. You may be resisting the effort it takes to establish better communication in the family.

If someone in the family is talking about a topic you find uninteresting, you may say so and suggest a shift to a mutually enjoyable topic. But beware of boredom which says, "Go away. Don't bother me" to a family member. Your attitude may convey such a message even when your words do not.

In a friendly tone, you may say, "I'm really not interested in the play-by-play. Can't we talk about something else?" or "I really want to know what you've been doing, but not in such great detail." Statements such as these will tell of your continued interest in the person despite your disinterest in the topic.

Hidden Communication

Messages are flowing back and forth between people all the time, even when no words are being spoken. Visualize people lined up at work, each at a desk or at a machine in a factory. Each one is very busily engaged in his or her own task, looking neither to the right nor the left, but concentrating. You might say that they are not communicating with one another, but messages are going forth all the time. The most common one is, "I'm working hard; don't disturb me." But there are many variations:

"I'm falling behind! Come and help me." This worker has a pile of papers or other evidence of the task and is making very little progress in reducing it. He or she may glance at the unfinished work often, with an expression of helplessness.

"I'm really getting the hang of this now; I can do it faster." This worker is smiling slightly, moving quickly.

"Isn't it break time yet?" That would probably be the unspoken message of someone who just looked at the clock.

Similar messages are in the air at home. Father reading the evening paper silently may in fact be saying, "Don't bother me." Mother watching TV may be saying the same thing. However, the teenager standing quietly in the doorway may be asking, "May I come in and ask you for something?"

As an example of the kind of communication that gets transmitted unknowingly, I will quote the words of Marcia, who was telling me about the climate at her house:

> I don't know where my dad's at with money. My mother's so—she's not tight, she just doesn't like to spend, except on what she wants. Neither of them spends a lot of money. I think if my dad wanted to have a bigger house, he could afford pretty much what he wants. Sometimes I get the feeling that he's a millionaire and he's not telling me. Money is like a sacred subject, I mean real money, not just how much I've got in my pocket. You never hear about what your father's yearly income is and what he has in the bank.

Marcia is eighteen; she works and handles her own money. She's not complaining that she wants the money, just that she'd like to know more about the family's position.

The message Marcia is getting is that she is somehow unworthy of her parents' confidence, their trust. They have no idea that they are conveying such a message, but they are doing so by their failure to speak openly about a very important aspect of family life.

Another example of hidden communication occurs when

parents carefully hide their disagreements from their children. Their intentions are usually to spare their children the sounds of their fury, but what often happens is that the young people are fully aware of the fighting going on and draw inappropriate messages from their exclusion. Youngsters may feel that the parents are plotting to leave or are conspiring against them or that they are being excluded from an important event. As Dr. Dreikurs said many times, "Children are keen observers, but rotten interpreters." When they arrive at the teen years, their powers of observation are still keen, but their interpretations have already formed a pattern. The impact of the hidden communication is heavy upon them and they are no more likely to feel free to question.

Some very powerful messages are being transmitted all the time that are not as easy to recognize as those described above. The way we use our bodies, how we move, and how we sit and stand all work to send messages. Consider the powerful effect of walking out of a room. That is a method of communicating a strong message. It can have many meanings and is subject to interpretation by whoever is left behind. Perhaps you're familiar with Dr. Dreikurs advice for parents of younger children. When sisters and brothers fight, it is generally for the purpose of gaining the parents' attention or keeping parents busy with the children. If a mother or father walks away from the room where the children are fighting, they will understand that their parents choose to ignore the fighting and will change their behavior accordingly. To walk out of the room is to send a strong message, and it is a step to be taken only when you are quite certain of your own purpose in doing so.

This particular advice is just as useful in dealing with fighting between adolescents. It may be more difficult and it may take longer, but it is important for parents to recognize that each sibling is capable of deciding for himself or herself whether or not to keep up the conflict. There is no need for a parent to act as judge or mediator.

There is only one way to overcome the possible bad effects of hidden communication, and that is to establish spoken communication between and among all members of the family so that doubts, fears, and questions find a suitable climate in which to be aired and so that parents and children together can seek answers and information on the topics that concern them.

One of the most effective ways to establish such open communication is through the technique of the family council, which is explained in the next chapter.

6
Partnership

In order to achieve harmony in the household, it is important first to realize that family living has to be a partnership. If you don't consider it a partnership now, you will inevitably discover that it is. It is a system in which everything that happens affects every member of the family to some extent. Too often parents behave as if a family were a dictatorship, and the discovery that they do not in fact have complete control comes as a shock.

Partnership means that all share in the responsibilities as well as the rewards of family living. All are not equal partners in everything, but each has a voice and a duty. In order for the partnership to function well, it must be enhanced by mutual respect; that is, respect by the parents for the children as persons as well as respect by the children of the parents and other elders.

Mothers especially often err in speaking of and thinking of the home as "mine" and expecting all other family members to recognize her ownership. The kitchen is not mother's sole possession, nor is its upkeep her sole responsibility. The furniture is not the parents' sole possession, nor are the other articles that must be used by the entire family. A distinction is drawn between spaces and articles that are the entire family's and those that are the personal property of one member. For example, the kitchen is not just mother's, but certainly her dresser drawers and the contents are her private domain. The automobile may be father's for use in business; he may not even own it. On the other hand, it may be a family possession, as is the furniture. If it is a family possession, it is reasonable that it be shared. If it is not, the limits must be clearly set.

In considering the principle of partnership, do not assume that this means parents surrender. When parents relinquish domination, this does not mean that they are expected to indulge their children in every wish, but it is important that the younger members of a family have an opportunity to express those wishes.

We often fail to realize how much separation into classes exists among family members. Separation into dominant and submissive, superior and inferior, aggressive and passive, smart and stupid, old and young, capable and inept, are a few of the pigeonholes we use. Not only do these separations put distances between parents and children but also between mother and father and between older and younger siblings.

There are dangerous assumptions regarding the functions we expect of one another. Without realizing their errors, in many households members assume certain defined roles: father the final authority; mother the manager of the household; oldest sibling to be teacher, guide, model, and baby sitter for younger child; and youngest to be the recipient of service and attention. Although this assumption is mostly unconscious, it does impede the formation of partnership, and the first step in the shift is to become aware of it. It is necessary first to examine the way family members regard one another in order to make any effective changes. Especially today when sex roles are undergoing continuing change, it is important to recognize the boundaries of the individual roles and to work at opening and expanding them.

For instance, in some households mother is actually the final authority as well as the manager, while father has a minor role. Another household may operate with only one parent. Or a younger child in a family may catch up and overtake an older sibling. Thereafter that sibling, having shown increased ability, will be expected to continue to be the leader. Each son or daughter seeks his or her place in the family in a different way, and other family members adapt individually to one another as each one develops his or her unique personality.

The Family Council

One of the ways to attain mutual respect is to put into action the concept of equality through the technique of the family council. It can serve as the stage on which different roles are rehearsed, giving family members the opportunity to relate to one another in new ways.

In the book *Family Council,* the family council is described as follows:

A group of people who live together, whether or not they are related by blood or marriage. The group shall have regularly scheduled meetings and operate under rules agreed upon in advance. The meeting shall be an open forum at which all family members can speak without interruption, with freedom of expression,

without fear of consequences, and without regard for
age or status. Its deliberations result in decision only
when all members present agree—that is, come to a
common understanding. *

At stake is the relationship between and among family
members. The categories that divide the members must be
put aside, at least for the duration of the meeting. In this
way, responsibilities as well as rewards can be more equally
shared. In a family with teenagers it is especially essential to
have a family council, for it helps them to express their independence and contribute their ideas while at the same time
providing training in cooperation. With more experience in
living and participating outside the family, teens generally
have many more ideas to bring to the family council than do
the younger children.

The most effective family councils don't start that way.
They grow out of the attempts of all family members to learn
to cooperate and contribute. To begin, it is only necessary
for at least two members of the family to choose a convenient time and a comfortable place to hold the meeting and
invite the others. Especially with teenagers, it may be difficult to find a time when everyone in the family is free to
come, but it is essential that no obstacles are created that
might impair the beginning efforts. When the family is
gathered, discuss the purpose of the council and begin to
work on ground rules that everyone can accept. These would
cover the frequency of meetings, the time and duration, what
leadership to choose, and what topics are appropriate.
Generally a chairman and a secretary are necessary at each

*Dr. Rudolf Dreikurs, Shirley Gould, and Dr. Raymond J. Corsini, *Family
Council* (Chicago: Henry Regnery, 1974), p. 7.

meeting, the chairman to help keep order and the secretary to record decisions. As early as possible decide how the officers' terms are to be rotated. It's a good idea to rotate on a regular basis, so that even the youngest family member has a turn at being chairman and a turn at secretary. If the young child doesn't yet know how to write, he or she may appoint a substitute for the sole purpose of doing the writing.

The rules with which you begin ought to be as simple as possible. Start with easy questions, such as, "What can we do together after the meeting to have fun?" After the family has learned to get together on a regular basis and treat one another as cooperating equals, it will be feasible to deal with the tough questions that face every family. If parents look upon the family council meeting as the time to criticize and preach, their offspring will recognize the subterfuge and refuse to come. If, however, for the duration of the meeting both parents and any other adults treat each family member with respect and consideration, family council will become a very effective way for the family to be a source of support for each member.

The book *Family Council* mentioned in the preceding pages has explicit instructions and transcripts of actual families holding meetings. You may wish to refer to it to learn more about the subject.

When you have difficulty in the family council, as you are bound to, a good way to discover the actual problem is to apply the yardstick of equality and to ask: Is this the way equals would relate to one another? Is this the way a decision would be reached among equals? Is this the way equals would speak to one another? Is this the way equals would tackle this task?

This immediately makes clear what is going on and what can be done about it. If the people meeting together were friends instead of relatives, would they allow the oldest to have the final word? Would they expect any one person to shoulder the responsibility for getting the job done? Would they be reminding one another of past failures or past omissions?

With these concepts in mind, the family council becomes a true open forum for everyone in the family. Providing for the needs of all members ceases to be one member's sole responsibility and becomes instead part of a process in which everyone participates. Getting the chores done, the garbage out, and the dog fed ceases to be the task of those who would grudgingly perform those duties and becomes part of the process of keeping the family functioning.

When previous assumptions are questioned, new strengths arise. For example, the mother who is accustomed to being the manager of the kitchen and the household may discover that there is other managerial talent available. Perhaps her husband enjoys cooking and would rather have some kitchen responsibilities than others he currently assumes. The father who sometimes feels that all the responsibility for making decisions falls on his shoulders can discover that one arrived at jointly may be more valid. Brothers and sisters can learn to see one another—as well as their parents—in a different light. It may not be a rosy light, but it will be a clearer one. And this clear vision will produce a more harmonious relationship.

The following is transcribed from a recording of an actual family meeting. The Marshall family had been meeting together for some time, had studied Adler's and Dreikurs's methods, and were ready to tackle a sensitive subject. Mr. and Mrs. Marshall were both present, with Lisa, aged sixteen; Trent, aged fourteen; and Wallace, aged thirteen. This is excerpted from the meeting in progress (Lisa is chairman):

CHAIRMAN: Is there any other financial business?

FATHER: I'd like to know why I can't leave my loose change on top of my dresser and why I can't leave money in my billfold and expect that the next time I look it will be there. It's a very regular thing, day after day. I never know how much money I have. I think I have money in my billfold, and I go to pay for something and there's nothing there. The last time there had been about fifteen dollars, and then it was empty. I was embarrassed.

WALLACE: I've taken a few dimes and nickels. It was there on the dresser and I really needed it.

FATHER: I don't remember that we reached an agreement that my money was just available for anybody to help them solve their own problems.

MOTHER: You evidently assumed that I was taking money for parking meters, and I told you I never took any of your change, ever.

FATHER: I didn't assume anything like that.

MOTHER: I don't know what you assumed, but at any rate, you asked me what was happening to your change.

FATHER: I only assumed that I knew how to find out.

MOTHER: Well, I'm saying: No, I do not ever take any of your change.

FATHER: It really isn't the money that bothers me so much. It's two other things: one, an invasion of my privacy; the second is just the plain gross inconvenience of thinking I have money and then getting some place and finding I don't. I don't see why I should have to look in my billfold before I put it in my pocket to see if my money is still there.

TRENT: Well, I suppose it happened the time I needed money to go get some groceries.

FATHER: It isn't any one time. It's happened many many times.

WALLACE: Oh, I took some money one time—a couple times maybe. Two dollars last week that mother told me to take.

MOTHER: That mother told you to take?

WALLACE: Yes, to get some mix and some other stuff at Baker's.

MOTHER: I told you to take money out of dad's billfold?

WALLACE: Yes, because you didn't have any.

MOTHER: Well, I don't seem to have any recollection of that.

WALLACE: I do.

MOTHER: What can we do about it?

FATHER: I make a motion that we have a petty cash fund somewhere—say ten dollars that we could keep in change and periodically replenish it so that you'd all have some place to turn rather than my billfold. It seems to me that almost every day somebody is frantically dashing around looking for money.

MOTHER: I think that's a good idea, but I'd like to know what it's going to be used for. Does that mean that if people don't have enough allowance money left over they can just take what they need out of the petty cash fund?

FATHER: Well, I thought if somebody wanted to use it for their own purposes they'd put in an I.O.U. to replace it later.

MOTHER: It'd be fine if they would do that. Because there are some things we have to get for the household.

FATHER: To pay the paper boy or something like that.

WALLACE: Okay, I agree to that. Where should it be?

MOTHER: Where should we keep it?

TRENT: How about on that table in the hall?

FATHER: There's a motion before us.

TRENT: I second the motion.

CHAIRMAN: All in favor of having a petty cash fund, say "Aye." All respond "Aye."

CHAIRMAN: Any opposed?

(*No response.*)

CHAIRMAN: Then the motion carried. How are we going to do it?

FATHER: I suggest we appoint someone to find an appropriate container and a convenient place for it.

WALLACE: Can I do it?

MOTHER: Let me just say that I don't want any money put in any of the good china dishes. That's the only request I have.

CHAIRMAN: Okay, is there any more financial?

Words on paper convey only part of the relationship among the members of the Marshall family. All the discussion was carried on in reasonable tones of voice. No one shouted at anyone else, and no accusations were made. A solution was found for the problem presented. In order for family council to be most effective, it must meet the basic criteria of equality, mutual respect, open communication, regularity of meetings, agreed rules, joint deliberation, reciprocal responsibility, and mutual decision.

Peaceful Partnerships

Vertical relationships occur when there is a top authority and other family members take positions further down the ladder. *Horizontal relationships* exist when there is mutual respect and a feeling of equality as persons. Vertical relationships imply and enforce competition. Everybody is trying to climb the ladder, and the one on top has to keep pushing the others down. The people on the ladder have to use all their available energy competing for position. Horizontal relationships allow each individual to function actively without fear of losing his or her place. There is cooperation and greater productivity among them.

Partnership needs a horizontal plane on which to function. In some family relationships we use the vertical standards while we try to create a horizontal situation. For example, mother may assume that it is only natural that father has the last word, since he brings in the financial support. She fails to question the connection. True, without the financial support the family would be greatly inconvenienced, but does that necessarily give father the authority over what another family member may do or say or be? When children reach their teens, parents learn that they do not in fact have the final authority; the pain and shock of this discovery can be avoided or at least alleviated by the recognition of the actual relationship.

We err if we assume that some activities necessarily take precedence over others or that one person's wishes carry more weight than another's. Each person can control only his or her own actions. Equals do not force others to do their bidding; equals do not issue edicts to one another; equals do not punish one another or make unreasonable demands upon them.

Partnerships don't always operate smoothly, whether in business or in personal life, but family living functions best when all family members share fully. Family council, as an ongoing activity of the family, will help to improve the operation.

7
Setting an Example

Every moment of your life you act as a model for someone else. Your words and your activities become an example for the people with whom you are in contact, whether at work, at home, or circulating in the larger world. This is especially true and significant in relationships with adolescents, who are still forming their ideas about themselves and the world and how they should live in it.

No matter what you say, the impact of what you do is likely to be stronger. The old motto "Do as I say, not as I do" did not come about accidentally, for whoever originated it realized that his or her intentions could be loftier than his or her activities. It is questionable whether the admonition is ever successful. When one hears it, it is almost automatic to wonder why the speaker doesn't follow his or her own advice.

When we think we are telling our children what they ought to do or what's right or how things ought to be, they are quick to label such remarks as lectures or sermons and to disconnect their listening apparatus. Parents cannot impose one code for their children and live by another one themselves. Offspring will not follow orders if they feel like rebelling and certainly will not live by a code of ethics or morals if it is merely imposed and not demonstrated. This applies particularly to cheating in school, drinking, driving, and sexual behavior.

It is almost impossible to maintain pretense when living with adolescents. Smaller children may be confused by what they see if it isn't the same as what they hear, but adolescents will protest if they are required to follow a code of behavior that differs widely from the one by which they see their parents live.

Whose Values Will Prevail?

Most of us want our children to be better than we are. We try as parents to provide all the advantages and all the resources that we can in the hope that we will thus enable our children to have better lives. It rarely occurs to us to examine what that means. "Better" to one person may not mean "better" to another, for we place different values on the qualities of life. Usually values are not chosen but, rather, absorbed by each of us in our normal development. Until recent times we did not question the worth of the ideas we adopted from our families, our religions, and our society. The very nature of values causes us to accept our own as the only correct ones and to evaluate all others according to that standard.

This attitude creates conflict of varying degrees. For example, while a parent places a high value on keeping one's person and one's possessions clean and neat, the adolescent may see no worth in keeping the lawn cut, hair trimmed, or clothes clean and pressed. Similarly, a parent may place a high value on achieving a leadership position in an organized group while the teen sees no particular advantage to be gained through making an effort to achieve such a position.

If you live in a homogeneous community in which everybody has the same kind of house or apartment, where everybody wants the same things and follows similar political and social affiliations, it is easy to believe that there is really only one set of values and that people either live up to them or do not. There are variations in how well people perform, but it is assumed that everybody holds the same standards and expects to be rated thereby.

We are not called upon very often to examine our values, and we usually don't realize how we got them, but it is rewarding to discover what truths we hold and what we do about them. A clarification of the values we hold as individuals can be helpful in liberating us from the struggle to uphold those which are actually irrelevant. To discover what is most important is to become free to devote our time and energy toward attaining those standards instead of exhausting our efforts on less vital concerns.

In family life, parents show by their own lives what they actually value, even while they may preach a different standard. They may say, "It doesn't matter how well you do; what matters is how hard you try." But they may really believe that it's best to be first and may have transmitted this belief unknowingly. I watched Frank Ellison, aged fifteen, play a tough tennis match against an opponent who had vastly more experience in tournament play. Frank's father watched every move and made notes. When Frank came off the court, exhausted, Mr. Ellison immediately recounted all the specific moments when Frank might have saved points and improved his score. He repeated the motto about trying hard in an effort to convince his son that it was all right that he lost, but his attitude clearly showed that winning is all.

Truth vs. Reality

One parent always told her children, "Honesty is the best policy" and "We must always be honest with each other in the family." But the teens in that family have observed over the years that their mother buys an outfit and hides the sales check so she can tell their father it cost less than it did, and their father lies about how much he lost at playing poker. They have also observed the small lies that go on all the time when their parents wish to avoid certain people. Although parents may explain the difference between a real lie and a white lie, during the teen years young people are forming their own ideas about such distinctions and may not agree with their parents' rationalizations.

A parent may say, "Don't judge a book by its cover" and in fact expend great energies in keeping up a good appearance. The maxim "Love thy neighbor" is often quoted to young people by their parents. But those parents will be highly critical of friends their sons and daughters choose if those friends do not meet with parental approval.

Parents who never accept what someone else says may think they are demonstrating healthy skepticism. They engage in endless arguments that they call discussions. They show that it is very important to be right, and that unless you are right, you are defeated.

Another axiom to which many people say they give respect is "It doesn't matter whether you win or lose; it's how you play the game." But in everyday actions the mother who plays tennis will speak in triumph of the games she won, and the father will talk at length about the new stroke that is lowering his golf score.

The behavior of a young person reflects the attitudes and values of the parents. When those values are clearly defined and accepted by both parents, it is likely that their children will adopt them. When there is disagreement between the parents or between what either parent says and what he or she does, the adolescent will select the attitudes and values which seem constantly being used without the individual's awareness.

To learn how we choose our values and how our children acquire theirs is a subject for another volume. For the purpose of learning the behavior that will help achieve greater harmony with your adolescents, it is necessary only to become aware of the values you hold and the ways in which you are transmitting them. It's easy to acknowledge love, duty, patriotism, and religion as being of high value. It's harder to recognize the abstract values that you support.

In some families, the values transmitted are: to be strong, to be sensitive, to behave correctly, to be well known in the community, to have influence on others, to excel at whatever one undertakes; or on the other hand, to struggle, to lean, to conform to the expectations of others, to be extremely cautious. In a healthy family some of the values transmitted are: respect for other persons; trust in one another; cooperation before competition; participation and contribution to the ongoing work and enjoyment of the community of which one is a part.

Parents as Models

If the example you see yourself setting isn't the one you want your adolescent to adopt, what can you do about it? As with many other of life's difficulties, the first thing you can do is to think about it. What are you doing that you don't want your son or daughter to do?

Do you eat more than you know you should? And do you hear yourself telling your adolescent son or daughter to eat less junk food and cut down on desserts?

Do you occasionally have a few too many cocktails but worry that your teen will be brought home drunk one night?

Do you quarrel often with your friends while trying to tell your children to get along better with others?

Do you habitually drive beyond the speed limit but attempt to impress your son or daughter with the necessity to obey the law?

It is clear that you cannot impose a code of behavior for your children while you follow a different one. You may think you outwit them, but in the long run you can't. Each person growing up will adopt the values that make sense at the time, in accordance with the lifestyle of the individual and with the assortment of standards he or she meets.

If you are reading this book with the desire to achieve greater harmony in your household, then one value you hold is that of attaining harmony in the family. In that case, you can do the following to achieve your goal:

1. Realize how powerful is the example you set in the way you live your own life.

2. Examine the values you really hold.

3. Decide which of your values are most important to you and which you might restructure.

4. Prepare to consider and accept values different from your own.

There is no harm in stating your own values clearly; in fact, it is helpful to the struggling adolescent to know exactly where his or her parents stand. Nor do you have to acquiesce in values your children bring home when they are radically different from yours. But if you wish to stay friendly with them, you must accept their rights to have different values from yours. In order to do this, recall how your own values during adolescence differed from those of your parents and how the values you held at that time have shifted through the years, sometimes without your being aware.

Decide whether it is more important that your teens agree with you and adopt your values or that each of them develops fully as an individual. Freedom to differ with parents often opens the way for a young person to develop in constructive ways that a parent cannot foresee. Similarly, the parent who engages in constant efforts to persuade an adolescent that he or she should adopt the parent's values often succeeds only in creating distance and distress in the relationship.

One of the areas in which parents and their teens are likely to differ is the standard of sexual behavior. To illustrate: Scott and Karen, college students, were visiting Scott's parents, the Browns. In the course of conversation, Scott mentioned that Karen had come to visit him the preceding weekend on campus and that she had stayed in his room. Although the statement was not defiant, the Browns had not expected it and did not approve. Mr. Brown said, "I don't think that's such a hot idea at your ages." He was trying hard not to be punitive. Scott replied, "You don't have to like it. You don't even have to approve. We just didn't want to lie about it."

Different standards and different values make it impossible for the two generations always to agree, but it isn't necessary that they must. What is necessary is that each feels free to state his or her position on an issue, in an attitude of respect for one another as individuals. When people differ, they don't have to put one another down just because they disagree. To hold different standards is not to be an inferior person.

There will be many clashes during the course of the teen years, many times when the younger persons challenge the ideas and ideals that their parents hold precious. At the same time, the parents are likely to be questioning some of their own values and finding it difficult to know which ones to hold and which to modify.

The age of everyone receiving a code of behavior from parents and preachers and holding to it throughout life is gone. There isn't even much use any more for the etiquette books, because they can't keep up with the accepted changes in human behavior.

When you examine a value you hold, see if you can figure out why it's dear to you. Is it because of what other people might say or think? Is it because without it your life would be unbearable? Or is it more habit than anything else, a habit you could break if it meant a better relationship with someone else?

In reaching for greater harmony, however, do not feel you must give up everything you stand for and succumb to the new ways of the younger generation. What you must do is to decide for yourself what is really important to cling to and what is open to question. You cannot control which of your values your children will adopt, but you can get a clearer picture in your own mind of where you stand and where you draw the line. All relationships aside, such an evaluation is at least bound to help you grow as an individual.

8
Dealing with Conflict

You don't have to have those fights around the house. You don't have to give in, but you don't have to win either. Even when you all disagree, which happens often, the disagreement does not have to escalate into a screaming, fighting match. You can cope successfully with the conflict if you can implement the following:

1. Reduce the conflict to the actual issue
2. Respect the other persons
3. Respond with a search for agreement
4. Renew the sharing of responsibilities

When young children fight, parents often act as mediators. A parent is called upon to decide who is right and who is wrong, who shall have the toy and who shall be told to give it up. More often a parent is called upon to decide which television program is to be shown. In their innocence, parents feel that this is their proper responsibility and do not realize that the fight between and among the children is usually created for the specific purpose of getting mother or father, another adult, or all of them involved. Each child wants to show his or her power over the parent, and the parent falls right into the trap. The child who can enlist father on his side and say, "Dad says I'm right" has exerted his power not only over his sibling but over his father, who has been made to take sides between his children.

When children are older, the opportunities for arguments are greater, and the disagreements are more difficult to settle. Everything in their lives has grown in scope: their abilities, their responsibilities, their very body size reminds them and their parents that they are now nearing adult stature and will no longer accept the treatment they received as children. The conflicts over toys now relate to the use of the car; the conflicts over bedtime now relate to curfew time. With the increasing mobility and independence of teenagers, parents have less and less control over their sons' and daughters' activities and more occasion to preach virtue and issue orders.

Disagreement: Major or Minor?

Conflict can erupt over anything at any time. What is a simple decision in one family can become a major confrontation in another. In the Lopez family, Juan, aged fourteen, was in conflict with his grandfather because he wanted to take part in activities at his school that would keep him away from home until 9:30 P.M. Juan felt he was being entirely reasonable, since his parents had encouraged him to participate in the folk festival for which rehearsals were held in the evening. Grandpa, a recent immigrant, felt that no respectable child should be out in the evening without his parents. The parents, caught between the old and the new, wisely decided that Juan could continue, especially since he was a good student, well behaved, and respectful. In making this decision they treated their son with respect and trusted him to keep his word.

Mike Gardner, aged fourteen, had a different problem concerning staying out late. His parents wanted him to learn the value of a dollar, so he got a job as a busboy in a restaurant near his home. It was close enough so that he could ride his bike there; he didn't need to ask anyone to drive him to work. However, he didn't want to leave work until the restaurant closed, because the longer he stayed the more tips he could make. His parents wanted him home by ten o'clock, but he continued to stay there until midnight. At home, his father and mother often scolded him about his keeping late hours. His schoolwork suffered and his disposition became sullen. Finally, one night he fell asleep on the job and was fired. His parents felt they had won a battle, but Mike felt that even if he lost, he proved he could defy them. No attempt had been made to reach any kind of agreement; Mike and his parents were each trying to prove who was boss.

Conflicts with teens affect the whole family. Mother and father may disagree, each taking a different side in the battle, and sometimes the problem threatens the marital relationship as well as the parent-child relationship. Brothers and sisters will also have opinions and preferences, even when they do not actively take part in the fighting. Any tension aroused by the bickering can affect any other aspect of the lives of the individual family members.

Conflict Pervades the Family

It may be hard to see the connection between an argument that seems to involve only one adolescent and the effect that argument has on another sibling. In the Connor family each member was affected the night Bruce, aged seventeen, stayed out until 4:00 A.M. with the family car. His father and mother were both awake when he came in and ready to do battle. Father's approach was autocratic ("Don't you dare stay out that late ever again!") and demeaning ("What kind of a bum are you?"). Mother's approach was that of the injured parent: "How could you do this to me? I was so worried about you!" The arguments lasted for an hour until the three exhausted themselves and each other and retired.

The next morning Bruce's sister Mae, aged fourteen, couldn't go to Sunday school. She had an upset stomach, which was promptly diagnosed as "a touch of the flu." Her parents didn't realize that Mae was affected by the fighting. They knew she was a really good girl who disapproved strongly of her brother's behavior. It didn't occur to them that she was listening to every word, worrying about her own freedom. She wanted to continue to be her mother's favorite and wondered how much she would be restricted. Mae wanted to be the peacemaker when she heard the fighting, but she didn't feel that she could. It was the intensity of the feelings that contributed to her illness.

It is an error to assume that conflict in part of the family affects only the family members who actively participate in the conflict. The family is a system in which everything that happens has some effect on each of its members.

Consider how family fights develop. Nobody has to fight unless he or she wants to. At some moments it seems impossible to make peace. Feelings are hurt, personal prestige is injured, rights are trampled on, and the impulse comes to lash out, to attack, to avenge the wrong. But the fact is *we usually fight about something other than the real issue.* We fight about what has happened—what was said and done—in the mistaken idea that this will clear the air so things will settle down.

But the issue is not how late the teen returned home, who was supposed to do the dishes, or the money that was missing. The issue lies in the relationship among the people. It involves concepts of authority and superiority, winning and losing. If the conflict is to be resolved in a useful manner, the underlying issue must be discovered and considered. Harsh words don't help, nor does it help to bring up old grievances. The apparent source of conflict must be laid aside in order to expose what the participants are really fighting about.

Each person fighting has a purpose. It may be expressed in feelings such as these:

"He can't get away with this; I must show that I have control. This time I won't give in."

"I have to stay on top. My authority depends on my superiority."

"I'll show him how it feels. Revenge will be sweet."

"I'm tired of this; I won't put up with it any more. They'll see how they can get along without me."

"She must do what's right. There's only one right way, and I know what it is."

"He doesn't appreciate me. I give too much."

In all of those reactions are elements of antagonism: There is confrontation, competition, comparison, and control. None of them has any useful place in solving conflicts of human relationships. Each one makes it harder for people to accept and understand one another. A movement for superiority is reflected: a striving for one person to have power over another or to prove that he or she is better than the other.

In any conflict there is the possibility of winning, retaliating, controlling, judging, measuring; but there is also the possibility of losing, being defeated, feeling crushed and unworthy. The winner has a moment of triumph but must guard against the next round, for the loser will seek another chance to win. Even the person who acts like a victim, accustomed to being the loser, uses that stance to put others in his or her service, and thus the fighting goes on.

Solve It; Don't Avoid It

To find a way out of conflict, one must first ask whether the other person is less worthy of our respect and consideration because of a different point of view. It isn't usually the topic that makes the fight; it's the individual attitude toward it and the individual feelings at stake. While the fight goes on, everybody involved is cooperating to keep it going. To achieve a conclusion, only one person needs to quit fighting. This does not mean surrender. When you stop fighting and start thinking, you can examine your own participation and see what you yourself are fighting about. If you have some interest in prolonging the argument, try to find your own purpose. But if you want to bring it to a halt, start by saying so.

If you're trying to get control, realize that no one person can control another—and say so. The other people in the fight know it anyway. Nor can anyone else control you. In every action you do precisely what you intended to do, whether or not you realize it at the time.

If you're seeking superiority, that too is a futile effort. Each individual has his or her own worth and his or her own talents and strengths. In a democratic society each person has value. No one person is inherently superior to any other. To accept the equality of other human beings is to free one's self from continual striving for superiority.

If you're trying to keep score, remember that family life is not a boxing match to be measured by points gained. No one can be sure to be evenly matched, nor always to get fair treatment. It's more productive to deal with the situation—to seek a solution to a problem—than to decide in favor of one individual.

If you have in your mind a code by which you decide what's right, it would be best to spell it out, to write it down, and to see how many of your family members will agree to abide by it. If the rules are yours alone, it's pretty hard to impose them on others.

In trying to solve a family conflict, it's better for all family members to work together than for one to submit and feel aggrieved. Recognize that in order to reach an agreement, the *real* issue must be identified, all members must be treated with respect, and all must share the responsibilities for changing the situation. There is no special order in which these tasks need be done, since performance of each one contributes to the others. Every step toward any of them is a step away from the conflict.

To help get the family out of the fighting, all members need to be as involved in the solution as they are in the conflicts, but it can all start with just one family member who decides he or she doesn't want to fight because he or she doesn't want to win any more. Realizing what the fight is actually about, one person alone can understand what's going on and begin to act accordingly.

The family council, described in Chapter 6, is the ideal setting in which to discuss the family fighting and to explore ways to cope with it. At the moment of conflict, it is almost impossible to have a friendly discussion. Words at those times are weapons and the persons involved are at war. But at a quieter time, when there is no immediate battle, family members can talk about their differences and seek ways to establish respect for one another and find the areas of agreement they share. The discussion of responsibilities is also most productive when it is held within the family council.

It will take practice for family members to learn to deal with conflict in this manner and there will probably still be times when fighting will break out. Learning new ways to cope with family conflict, however, provides invaluable training for all family members to cope as well with other conflicts outside the home.

9
Courage To Be Imperfect

If you have or acquire the courage to be imperfect, you will be able to cope more successfully with the challenges of living. This specific feeling is an abstract concept that can be summoned and developed by every person. Stated very simply, it is the belief that you are a worthwhile person, even when you err.

What Does It Mean?

According to Webster's dictionary (third edition), courage means the "mental or moral strength enabling one to venture, persevere, and withstand danger, fear, or difficulty firmly and resolutely." To have such courage in one's own imperfection is to accept one's self as less than perfect but still of value. Because most of us believe that perfection is attainable, it takes great strength to admit that we make mistakes without feeling demeaned. Freed from the necessity to maintain an image of perfection, a person does not need to fear a loss of prestige through making a mistake. Mistakes then cease to be magnified and become merely incidents in the course of life.

What Are the Obstacles?

Because the concepts of democracy and social equality are relatively new, we still live as if there were some authority to set standards of perfection for us to meet. We try always to be right, disregarding the fact that others may not have the same concept of right that we do. In striving for perfection we become ambitious for superiority over others and feel inadequate when we fail. The obstacles lie in our measurements of ourselves and what we do, judging ourselves as falling short, expressed in terms like these:

"If only I:
    were better looking
    knew then what I know now
    came from a better family
    were a little older (or younger)
    had more (money, influence, charm)
                             . . . etc."

Such wishes are not likely to be fulfilled but act as roadblocks set up by the individual. They can be removed as one develops the courage to be imperfect.

What Does It Require?

To develop the courage to be imperfect requires the recognition that human imperfection is universal. Each of us will still be striving toward our own goals but without concentrating on the errors we make. Damage from an error results from the emphasis on it and the degradation of the person who makes it as much as from the effects of the error itself. A person must accept oneself as he or she *is*, good enough at *this* moment.

How Does It Affect the Parent-Teen Relationship?

If you, the parent, can show by your own example that you are able to make a mistake and learn from it, you will be demonstrating for your teen a healthy way to approach life's problems. If you don't expect your offspring to be perfect, you encourage them to accept themselves as they are, freeing them to function in productive ways. The example you set and the expectations you convey are the most important aspects of the relationships between the generations.

Marla Adams was a woman of achievement: a teacher, wife, mother of a teen and two younger children. She was always precisely well groomed and well dressed. Her standards were high and she met most of them but always felt as though she were behind in a race and couldn't catch up. She felt used and annoyed and frustrated that no matter how she tried she couldn't seem to do enough to gain appreciation from her husband and her children. When we discussed her goal to be perfect, she decided to test life without demanding perfection for a week. Whenever she became aware of her high expectations of herself or her family, she would consciously think about imperfection. The following week, she said, "If I don't have to be perfect all the time, I don't mind so much if Norton doesn't think I am." When she undertook to act to the best of her own ability at the time rather than to some outside standard, she was released from the feeling of losing a race.

Marla's seventeen-year-old son Vic noticed a change in his

mother that week and told me about it later, when acceptance of imperfection had already become part of Marla's life. He said, "For the first time in a long time, Mom didn't bug me about doing my homework, nor ask me if I walked the dog or took my vitamins. It was a lot more cheerful around the house."

Holding a hoop higher and higher might train an animal to jump through it, but holding standards beyond reach for yourself or your children only produces discouragement. Discouragement often shows up as laziness, sadness, moodiness, or ineptitude. Its opposite, encouragement, is a product of the courage to be imperfect and manifests itself as enthusiasm, cheerfulness, and productivity.

10
Pursuit of Success

Pursuit of success can bring upheaval during the teen years. Children who willingly ran hard in the quest for superiority, achievement, prestige, and popularity may decide that the running is too difficult, the success too elusive. If parents attempt to enforce standards of success that they hold precious, rebellion—and conflict between the generations—may result.

Even the child who has willingly worked hard all his or her life to earn the Scout badges, the invitations, the class honors and positions of leadership may decide that the racing is tiresome. Often this happens when a particularly successful person leaves a familiar situation for a new one, such as graduating from a junior high school as president of the class and entering a high school to learn that there are eight other past class presidents competing for president of the freshman class.

A story is told about the entering freshman class at one of the prestigious Eastern universities, where there are many applications each year for each opening. A professor first asks students to close their eyes; then anyone who was valedictorian of his or her graduating high school or prep school is asked to raise a hand. When the direction is given to open eyes, students are astounded to see that almost every hand in the room is up. Competition will be among top winners.

We are concerned with what this kind of striving does to family relationships and to the individual student. Usually the pursuit of success is shown very early in life as part of a great tradition. From the earliest competition over whose baby walks first or says a word first, through which one can read first, who wins more blue ribbons, and who has the first date, parents and teachers often stress the importance of winning at any cost. They say, "It isn't whether you win or lose but how you play the game"; but what they mean is, "Win any way you can, but be sure to win."

Even when adults realize that not everyone can win, they often belittle the person who doesn't. A man I knew used to say, "Aim for the moon so you shoot over the bushes." Others say, "You must do the very best you can!" Implicit in these remarks is the statement that the person to whom they are addressed probably can't make it to the top. The product of setting high goals can be discouragement both for the one who makes it and for the one who doesn't.

The one who makes it may feel, as Edwin "Buzz" Aldrin was quoted as saying, "After you've been to the moon, there's nothing else to aim for; it's all down." In addition, that winner may tie his or her own sense of worth to winning and feel discouraged when he or she does not. The other result is that the person who is tied to winning may limit his or her attempts to those fields in which he or she is sure to excel. Thus, the excellent scholar may eschew athletics and vice versa. The competent pianist may avoid playing games. All of us know people who say, "I only do the things I do well. I can't stand being second best."

We need not belabor the effect on the person who doesn't win and feels that he or she can't win. Discouragement prevents much productive effort; the energy that would be available is dissipated by the discouragement.

Perils of Cheating

There are additional results of excessive competition. Cheating in order to get high grades is epidemic. Scandals involving violation of the honor codes regularly emerge at the United States service academies, and many old established universities are reexamining honor codes that have been in existence for more than fifty or sixty years. Their students had found too many ways to cheat, and when confronted with evidence of cheating, claimed that pressure for high grades caused them to ignore the code of honor.

In Bill Raspberry's column in the Chicago *Sun Times* of July 11, 1975, he writes about his meeting with a college senior who was disturbed over the number of bright, well-educated young men involved in the Watergate scandals. He quotes the young man, who thought he knew why. "It's the educational system," he said. "It's geared toward cheating because of the pressure to succeed."

At the 1974 graduation of the University of Michigan Medical School, the class president, David Forst, spoke about the necessity to improve the education of physicians. He said:

> Every year academic criteria for admission are more difficult and competition is more severe. In premedical

training this is manifest by increased cheating on examinations, falsifying of experimental data, and unwillingness to assist fellow students. Unless we begin to reevaluate our admissions policies, a real danger exists that we will be producing future physicians whose humanitarian interests have been smothered by competition before they even begin medical school. Contest will replace compassion, technology will mute the art.

An even greater danger is seen by Dr. Darold A. Treffert, director of the Winnebago Mental Health Institute at Winnebago, Wisconsin. He has connected an increase in adolescent suicides with the pursuit of success. He quotes a teen who had always been a straight-A student. When she got a B on her report card, her parents were upset. The next day, her birthday, she hanged herself. In her note she wrote:

Mom and Dad have never said anything to me about having to get good grades. In fact, we rarely talk about it. But I know they do not want, nor could they tolerate, a failure. And *if I fail in what I do, I fail in what I am.* *

It is easy to deplore the emphasis on high grades and the cheating that sometimes results. It is harder to find ways to prevent it and possibly hardest to examine the values on which cheating is based. The only way cheating can be abated is to release the pressure on winning at any cost. We must convince ourselves and one another that each child, adolescent, and adult has his or her own intrinsic value as a person, not dependent on the number of awards or the achievement of high grades. Only when a student is

---

*Darold A. Treffert, M.D. "Happiness is . . . the American Dream." *Inspection News,* vol. 60, no. 3, Fall 1975 (italics added).

thoroughly convinced of his or her own value, convinced that he or she is good enough, is that student free to study, to learn, to participate, and to contribute. The tension that builds in the person who is not secure in his or her own worth is often the very force that inhibits the use of one's full capacity in meeting a challenge, whether it be a speech, an exam, or a contest.

Danger of Prodding

Parents are afraid that if father and mother do not place sufficient stress on winning, on high grades, on awards, that their children may not strive. The opposite is true. When a parent says, "You could do better than that," the message is, "You didn't do well enough," and their child's interpretation is, "I didn't do well enough; therefore I'm not good enough." Anxious parents who place emphasis on success often contribute to the very discouragement that prevents their offspring from becoming successful. Each person responds much more effectively to the striving that comes from within than to the pressure that comes from others.

In a conversation I had with two high school seniors, one of them, whom I shall call Trina, commented on success in this way as she traced her own history from the time she entered school:

> I always used to think I liked school. In grammar school I didn't like to stay home because I would miss something. The work was so easy because I was a good reader, and I could do well in math, and there was nothing hard. Their system was so dumb. They were always handing out cookies to one kid that did well and gold stars to the other one who did even better. And

then the poor kid who didn't get any cookies feels awful, like he's a big dummy or some kind of a fool. Well, maybe he isn't such a dummy, and why should he be made to feel that way? I'd get cookies all the time and I'd feel like a big shot because I was in the advanced reading group. Now I only study if I want to, because I want to learn. Not for the cookies or the gold stars, or not in competition with someone else.

Trina's friend Roger, who was listening, was an outstanding student. Even so, he didn't approve of competition:

High school was just like a ladder, everybody trying to get on the top rung, and it made a mess. You couldn't pursue your own interests. The faculty people take you by the hand and tell you what you have to do. You don't learn much, except you learn how to cheat, to lie, to be competitive. You learn all sorts of things that don't help you to be a better person. You don't learn to satisfy yourself. In a competitive school, people are always comparing you with other people. I don't think it's good for a person to be always so apprehensive and anxious. If a person's apprehensive or anxious he's racing all the time in every direction, and can't really learn anything or accomplish much. Competition isn't good for motivation.

These two students had been high school dropouts in their junior year, and both returned to an alternative school a year later, so they were in effect comparing the traditional suburban achievement-oriented high school with a more open community-based school operated by their own district.

On the subject of how parents' attitudes affect what a student does, Trina said:

I don't ever want them to feel bad. Sometimes I think if they knew what I was really doing they'd be mad at me. I don't ever want to shame them or make them feel bad because they've never done anything to shame me. But I wouldn't be a cheerleader for my mother, or anything like that. She'd like to see me be happy, but she'd like it also if I would go to school and do the nice things. I know I don't always do the right thing, but I wish once in a while I could be commended for doing right, even though I know I shouldn't expect it.

Asked to describe how parents could treat their children in order to help them most, she said:

Especially when a child is little, and even as he gets older, try to accept almost anything their kid wants to do. Show a lot of enthusiasm for his interests, help him, and spend time with him.

Roger added:

Try not to hide, try not to be so vague. Don't try to live up to an image, but just really say and do what you feel in front of your kids. Try to raise your kids in total honesty. A kid is a person, and has the same feelings that everyone else has. Don't forget it. Parents should always listen, they should always accept. They don't have to agree, and they don't have to do what their kid says, but they should always accept his right to say it.

Just as children cannot live by the blueprints for life that some parents impose, it is just as impossible for any set of parents to live up to the expectations that their offspring see as ideal, and in fact it wouldn't be a good idea to try, but there's room for improvement in most relationships between parents and their children. In accepting what they do, parents show that they accept the teens who do it. When it is an illegal or unethical act, parents ought to be clear and outspoken about their disapproval. This means that if parents don't want their children to cheat, for instance, they must place heavier emphasis on honesty than on success. If they want their children to be law-abiding, they must be law-abiding themselves, and not privately enjoy their children's pranks while openly condemning the behavior.

Even when adolescents begin to look and act like adults, they are still in need of encouragement and acceptance from their parents. Sometimes in order to be encouraging to one's children an adult must first learn to accept his or her own imperfections. The man who never went to college may desperately want his son to distinguish himself in an academic career. The plain mother of a pretty daughter may expect her to be continually at work on her appearance in order to make the mother feel better. Either is an unfair burden for a young person to carry. He or she needs to be allowed to develop along the paths he or she chooses without regard for fulfilling the parents' old dreams.

Be cautious when you take an interest in your child's activities and achievements that your own self-esteem is not at stake. Often a parent will enter enthusiastically into the pursuit of musical study, for instance, and be crushed when the teen loses enthusiasm. Just as the child's worth does not depend on his or her own accomplishments, the adult's worth does not rest on the achievements of the children.

When you can lift the burden of meeting your own goals from your adolescent, you free that young person to pursue goals of his or her own choosing. Maintain an interest, be generous with encouragement, but limit your own investment. Your own self-esteem need not rise or fall with your teen's success or failure.

When success and failure are no longer the two poles for achievement, each person becomes free to use ability in a productive way, in cooperation instead of competition.

11
The Guilt Trip

Guilt surrounding an individual can be paralyzing. So many parents feel guilt in relation to their children that it often has the effect of making it impossible for them to function in a way that will actually be helpful both to the children and to themselves.

The feeling of guilt seems unavoidable, but it isn't. Most of us have had guilt foisted upon us from early childhood and feel that it is a valuable emotion that guards us from doing wrong. In many ways, it is. This is not to say that guilt is inappropriate in relation to a criminal act but, rather, that guilt has no place in relationships among family members. Guilt in itself cannot right a wrong, cannot undo what has been done, nor redo an improper act.

In relationships within the family, everyone can be freer to live in harmony when guilt disappears; and although there is no magic wand to make it disappear, we can examine it and try to understand it better than we do now.

Guilt: What Is It?

It's easy to acknowledge that guilt is a bad feeling; it's a "down" rather than an "up," a "low" rather than a "high." It is also a combination of other bad feelings, mainly the feelings of failure, shame, blame, and depression. In fact, it is difficult to separate them; they merge in different ways.

The feeling of failure may be expressed by the thought, "If only I . . . ." The rest of the sentence might be "knew better" or "didn't give in that time" or "listened to the advice I was given" or "kept my mouth shut." In every case, the feeling of failure results from something that happened in the past, something that didn't turn out just right. Your teen gets into an auto accident, for instance, after curfew. The damage is slight, and no one is injured, but you feel that it happened because of your own failure. If you had somehow been a better parent, it wouldn't have happened. This kind of guilt feeling is often expressed by: "Where did I go wrong?" "What did I fail to do?"

The feeling of failure may contribute to an unpleasant, even an awful, confrontation in which things are said that lead to more bad feelings between parent and teen. The feeling of failure—the guilt—has hampered the relationship between the generations and made it more difficult for everyone.

Shame is expressed by "What will they think?" The "they" may be the neighbors, the in-laws, the teachers, the boss, even the teen's sisters and brothers. Always implied in the feeling of shame is "What will they think *of me*?" The mental picture of shame may be connected to a shield from the gaze of others. The thought may be, "If I lie low and stay covered, maybe they won't notice my guilt." Certainly it's reasonable to be concerned about one's value to others, but shame doesn't help to increase that value.

When blame is connected to guilt the thought arises, "It's all my fault." Blame can be pointed at others, but when one has a feeling of guilt, there is blame on one's self. It's connected to a feeling of failure and implies that "if I were good enough, I wouldn't fail." Therefore, I blame myself for failing, for allowing this to happen.

Depression sums up the "down" feelings. It can, of course, be attached to other emotions besides guilt, but guilt feelings operate to make a person feel that "I'm not good enough, the world is too tough for me, I can't cope with my problems, and there is no hope."

Guilt arises in response to an occurrence. Some of the kinds of situations that bring forth guilt are:
• When something goes wrong;
• When someone else discovers your failure;
• When you violate your own goals;
• When you see yourself as you think others see you.

All of the feelings described are produced internally, and they need have no absolute correlation to what is actually going on. What we are concerned with here is the way guilt feelings affect your function as a parent. You may go along fairly smoothly for some time and even feel good about the way you handle your personal and family responsibilities, and then something happens that seems to upset your equilibrium. When you feel suffused with guilt, it's time to try to figure out why and what you're going to do about it.

What can guilt do to you? Among the responses that guilt may evoke from an individual are these:

To become defensive; that is, to offer reasons and excuses for whatever seems to be wrong.

To attack; to lash out at others, seeking to make others feel guilty, in the false hope that this will relieve your own guilt feelings.

To withdraw into silence, holding guilt feelings close inside and limiting interaction with others.

To weep, surrendering one's control and acknowledging total inadequacy.

Some persons may actually become physically ill as a consequence of heavy guilt feelings, and there is also the physical sensation of exhaustion that may follow an episode in which guilt has had a large part.

Emotion Has Purpose

What is the purpose of these guilt feelings? When one can understand the purpose, there is the greatest possibility to alter the feelings. Among the purposes of guilt, several main ones can be noted:

To control other people; the idea behind this purpose is that others will change their behavior in order to reduce one's own guilt.

To show how much one suffers; the mother who suffers so has become a stereotype in current fiction. This is not limited to mothers, however, but can be used by anyone in order to elicit appreciation from other people.

To punish one's self. Mixed up in this is the feeling of having failed, and the thought that if a person feels guilty enough, that will somehow make up for the way he or she failed. It suggests that there is some great scoreboard in the universe recording wins and losses, failure and atonement.

To get sympathy. When one does not feel adequate in a situation, one way to compensate is to get others to feel sorry for oneself.

To prove one's worth. This simple goal underlies all other aspects of guilt feelings. Guilt is mainly a sign of good intentions, an indication that "I know what's right and what success would require, and if I can't do it, at least I can show that I'm good enough to feel guilty."

The person who feels good enough doesn't have to bother with feeling guilty. That person has the courage to be imperfect and can accept a failing without undermining his or her own self-confidence. At times, all of us feel that we have not lived up to the standards we hold, whether they be moral, ethical, religious, or standards of achievement, but this does not imply that a· guilt feeling must follow. It is human to fall short, just as it is human to want to succeed, to want to live up to one's highest ideals.

Guilt feelings get in the way of the effective actions that can lead to improved relationships. Guilt feelings make it hard to do what needs to be done and keep us immobilized as if from some outside impairment. Once a person can realize that guilt is primarily a sign of good intentions, it becomes much easier to get rid of the guilt and get on with the task.

It is inevitable that accidents will occur, that conflicts will arise, that situations will entangle us, but it is not inevitable that any one of us must feel guilty in the process of coping. To remove the guilt feelings is to make room for the feeling of confidence, the ability to master the situation. It is not necessary to feel guilty in order to feel good, just as it is not necessary to feel superior in order to feel worthwhile.

12
Stepparenting:
A Special Problem

When parents separate, there is an effect on their children ranging from slight to severe. When they have already reached their teens, the children's personalities and preferences are fairly well formed. They have some understanding of the situation. They may not perceive it as you wish, but they draw their own conclusions and make the adjustments they feel are necessary.

Complications arrive in the remarriage of either parent. Even when one member of a new marriage has no natural children; even if one member of the new marriage has been single, the new family created by this marriage is an entirely different group from the one that existed before.

Loyalties are not easily broken or changed, trust is not quickly established, and the habit of respect for one another may not begin immediately.

Problems Compounded

Stan Hirsh was talking to me about the difficulties of maintaining a relationship with his teen-aged son, who lives with his mother. Stan was divorced from his first wife when the boy was seven and married again within the year. His new wife has custody of the three children from her first marriage, and they have a child together. Stan said:

> George doesn't get along with his mother. He never did, so she still expects me to discipline him. Now he's seventeen, and I could tell him all day long to be home at midnight, but I can't enforce it, because I'm not there. I don't have any control at all over my first set of children, and it hurts.

Marguerite Simmons also has a teen-aged son. She was divorced from his father when he was eight and married again the next year:

> My divorce was hardest on Lance. He had had the same friends since he was little, and it was hard for him to break away from them. Then he had to learn to live with a new father who liked an athletic son, and Lance is not athletic. I guess I'd made a lot of mistakes with him when he was little; he was so much like my first husband that I had to learn to deal with him in an entirely new way.

Joel is sixteen, his mother's only son. He has a natural sister and a stepsister. His parents divorced when he was nine, and both his mother and father were remarried in a very short time. He lives with his mother and stepfather. He speaks about his feelings:

> My father just didn't seem to care. My stepfather cares about me. My real father wants to start over what he's ruined all these years. It's too late. He forgot about us.

He left us totally fatherless. When he got married, we lost him. His wife is very nice, but since he got married, we hardly see him at all. It's terrible. You want to be close to your stepfather, but you don't want to leave your real father out. Then he has stepchildren too, and you don't know where you stand with them. It's so hard to explain. I know a kid who just got adopted by his stepfather; his real father can't ever see him again. I don't know what parents ought to do. It's not their fault if they don't like each other; they just don't realize what they're going to do to their kids. Almost all my friends have parents who are divorced or who're getting divorced. We're all about the same age. My parents got divorced first, and then Fred's, and then Dick's. Art's and Phil's were later. I guess parents get tired of each other, but I wish they could stay married. They ought to just plug up and not try to change each other, just try to accept how people are.

Although Joel speaks about parents in conflict, his advice is appropriate for all human relationships: Just try to accept one another as valuable human beings. Every person has some intrinsic worth, even though two people may decide they are not suited to one another for a lasting marriage. When two persons dissolve a marriage either or both of them hope to find in a new marriage the proof of their own ability to succeed. Sometimes the expectations placed on the new family are too high to be reached, and the cycle of conflict is repeated.

In the happiness of a new marriage, the parent who is new to the children may expect them to live up to exaggerated standards to fulfill his or her hopes. It is usually the father who is the new parent, since custody is most often awarded to the mother when a marriage is dissolved. On the other hand, he may have exaggerated fears connected with his new relationships. Either way, standards may be imposed that are unreasonable and particularly outrageous in a new and untried situation.

Trying Harder

The new father in such a household may feel he has failed to be an appropriate father to his natural children and try harder to prove he can be a good father to his stepchildren. If his method is to assert his authority and require instant obedience, he will most certainly meet opposition. He cannot expect teenagers to accept him and his orders wholeheartedly. They may continue to perceive him as an outsider and accept no orders. The best possibility for establishing a harmonious relationship with stepchildren lies in slowly building respect, trust, and cooperation. In order to build these qualities, the new parent as well as the continuing parent must practice them with the younger members of the household and be prepared for testing and questioning.

Still another relationship is created if the newly married parents have another child. The baby then becomes the symbol of the united family but at the same time adds another dimension to the complex relationships. Edie, aged fourteen, resents her new little sister. Edie's natural parents were divorced when she was nine. Edie had always been her mother's favorite and helper. Her physical appearance is naturally like her mother's, and she has copied her voice and even her gestures. She is accustomed to hearing compliments and was comparatively unruffled by the divorce and remarriage. She even enjoyed helping to care for her baby sister when she was tiny. Now that Sally is four years old, Edie sees her as a rival:

When Sally is around I can hardly watch TV. If I turn it on, she comes in crying, wanting something else. Then my mother runs in after her, saying, "What are you fighting with for her? Leave her alone. She's only a baby."

Edie's life is being disrupted by this competitor, for she is expected to indulge the younger one. In Edie's eyes, Sally has the best of all possible worlds—two parents who are united to protect her. Edie now feels as if she has been pushed aside in her family. Her parents' actions may in fact communicate that message. Only when the parents allow the sisters to form their own relationship will it be possible for them to enjoy one another and to cooperate instead of compete. Sally's parents are teaching her in these incidents that the way to get what she wants in the world is to cry for it and create scenes. Although only the one incident is described here, Edie cites many more in talking about her resentment of her younger sister.

When Edie's mother and stepfather learned to let Sally and Edie work out their own difficulties, the sisters had fewer conflicts and began to renew their bonds of affection.

Reaching One Another

Each person in a family has an individual relationship with every other person, and it is in error for a parent to try to command what that relationship is to be. When the new parent attempts to find his or her place in the affections of each stepchild, the biological parent errs in acting as a go-between. It is natural for the biological parent to want his or her children to see and appreciate all the good qualities of the new parent and ignore that which may not be desirable.

However, each family member will be forming impressions and making his or her own decisions about how the new relationships will develop and function. Speeches of praise or criticism do affect relationships, but not always the way the speaker intends.

For example, Mrs. Carter was distressed about the way her son and his new stepfather treated one another. They were polite but cool and distant and usually avoided one another. She tried hard to get both of them interested in a joint hobby, suggesting in sequence fishing, model building, and tennis. The harder she tried to find something to which they would both respond, the less they seemed to care.

Once when Mrs. Carter was away from home, Mr. Carter, whose hobby was photography, invited Ben down to his darkroom. As he worked, he explained what he was doing and gradually Ben understood the procedure and asked if he could help. By the time Mrs. Carter returned, her husband and her son had become enthusiastic partners in photography.

The crucial difference was that the stepfather and son found their common interest without the help of a third party. Mrs. Carter's intentions were good, but by attempting to initiate the idea for a joint hobby she made it harder for them to get together. It was apparent that they both wanted an activity they could share, but they didn't want it if it meant only pleasing her. Without her contrivance they were free to reach out to one another. Since she had not suggested photography, they ran no risk of disappointing her if their enthusiasm lagged. The photography project acted as an occupation through which they could become better acquainted and eventually led to a richer life for the whole family.

The relationship between any two persons is made up of perceptions, attitudes, and feelings, none of which is visible or tangible. All we can see is the behavior, the actions, and we hear the words and sounds of voices. Often we misinterpret what we observe. Human relationships remain changeable, however, and opportunities for improvement continue.

Although the foregoing comments refer to stepparenting, they apply to other family arrangements as well. Some of the variations are the family headed by one parent; a combined family that brought together two parents, each with own children; an amalgamated family into which a newly married pair bring a child of their own to join others born before the marriage. The adolescent years bring new stress to every family, and when for any reason teenagers do not live in a family headed by their first mother and father, the problems are compounded. Parents need to exert extra effort to resolve conflict and build harmony.

A word to the single parent: If you try to be both mother and father to your child or children, you will surely fail. Such great expectations of yourself only make it harder to be the one adequate parent you can be. You cannot protect your child or children from the reality of their own family situation, nor is it helpful to apologize to them for it. If you accept the limits that make your family somewhat different from the ideal, your children are more likely to do so.

For disrupted families as well as continuing ones, the same principles apply. Accept other family members as they are and work at becoming friends. Expect that there will be difficulties, especially as children become adolescent, and learn to work at solving them. Do not expect that life will be ideal or that your dear ones will be perfect. Expect that all family members will want to help make family harmony if they have the opportunity to do so in an atmosphere of care, consideration, trust, and respect.

13
Planning for the Future

During adolescence a young person moves from his or her parents' sphere toward his or her own. The source of much of the conflict between the young person and the parents is the direction in which that move is made. Parents naturally feel more experienced in the ways of life and thus more competent to plan for the future. They may overlook their teens' inner strivings or assume always that as parents they know best.

This may have been acceptable in earlier years of childhood and even in adolescence until recent decades, but as Chapter 1 has pointed out, the rate of change in the universe now is so rapid that no one set of parents can be sufficiently well informed to influence their offspring's decisions with wisdom.

Each adolescent needs at least a general plan for what he or she will do when compulsory education is finished. More and more young people are questioning the value of extended education, but it is not easy to find alternatives. Our culture appears to have decreed that young people do not have a significant place in the world outside the classroom. When jobs are scarce, it is among teens that the rate of unemployment is highest. They lack skills, they lack experience, and thus they're deprived of the opportunity to participate in the world of work.

The rate of discontinuance of education is increasing even among the middle class. Some students decide that conventional education does not suit them and leave school as early as the law allows. These are the "dropouts." Others are asked or forced to leave by school authorities because their behavior or achievement does not come up to expected standards. These are the "pushouts."

All of these situations are reported in the public press and are indicative of trends in family life and in public expectations, but the decisions that concern the parents of adolescents are the individual ones made by their own children.

Sometimes parents have clear ideas about what their offspring ought to do. Many fathers expect their sons to follow them into their trade or profession, or to take over a family business. Mothers of daughters sometimes find it hard to understand that today's young woman wants an independence her mother never craved and feels the need to prepare for it.

As in other aspects of family relationships, parents cannot successfully direct their children along the paths they wish them to follow but can only participate with them in reaching decisions if the family atmosphere is harmonious. If there is hostility between the generations, planning for the future is sure to bring out sharp disagreements as each parent and each teen strives to win, as described in Chapter 8. Although it is unlikely that complete agreement can be reached, parents can decide for themselves precisely what they will do to support the adolescent financially and emotionally, and even more specifically, define the limits beyond which they will not go.

There are four main tasks of adolescence listed in the introduction. We're concerned here with two: emancipating from parents, and choosing career goals. Within the choice of career goals lies the necessity for making decisions about preparation for that career, whether it be further education, apprenticeship, or work experience that is to be sought.

In most cases emancipation and separation from parents occurs at the end of adolescence. Whether it is in friendship or in anger depends largely on the kinds of relationships between the generations that have developed during adolescence. It is possible to limit parental obligations and still stay on friendly terms with your adolescents. It is in fact preferable. Children like to know where they stand with their parents and do not thrive in a situation where they must wonder about limits. As they grow older and closer to adult status they want to know what they can expect from their parents in terms of tangible assets and emotional support.

Moving Outward

The larger world opens to adolescents, and young people are faced with the challenge of making places for themselves "out there," of finding individual niches where there seem to be no openings. They have to find ways to make contributions in a world that seems complete without them. Doubt in one's own competence leads to discouragement that adds an additional barrier to be hurdled. On the other hand, young people who have had experiences in making appropriate decisions for themselves, of discussing with their parents matters of mutual interest, and of experiencing success in the outcome of their endeavors are equipped to take greater risks and larger steps toward maturity.

As soon as parents realize that they have very little control over what their children think and do, they can respect those young people as separate individuals, trust them, and spend their own energies in their own roles in making decisions. The groundwork for the decisions has already been laid in the past.

For instance, there is a set of values in each family, which has become evident to the children of the family long before they reach adolescence. Even little children notice whether their parents read or watch television. They are aware of their parents' interest in the world outside the family and whether it is limited to enjoyment and recreation or encompasses concern for their fellow man. Generally they know how much education their parents have had and of what use it is to them. They know the relative importance of money in the household. They may not know how much there is, but by adolescence they have very strong ideas about how it's handled and for what it's used.

It is futile, then, to attempt to convince young people to pursue specific goals if the parents do not. There isn't any power behind "you ought to" but there can be stimulation with "I wish you would." Events of recent years have demonstrated that there is no insurance to guarantee that our children will become adults according to the models we present. No matter how we choose their schools and their neighbors, no matter what kind of training we provide, the possibility exists that any one of them will choose a path in life of which we do not and cannot approve.

Of course, most do pursue a pattern that parents can accept, and therein lies the necessity to create and to maintain a harmonious relationship, not only for the satisfaction of parents but so that the young people can feel secure in the friendship and emotional support of their parents.

Making Decisions

In helping one's youngster to make decisions about his or her future, the first thing a parent can do is to listen to an offered idea. It may sound absurd, impossible, outrageous. But just as soon as a parent labels it so, its value in the eyes of the teen increases. The risk for the parent is that an argument will erupt over who knows best, and the merits of the idea will become buried in hostility. No longer will the idea itself be open to question because the issue will shift to who wins. However, the parent who listens and refrains from criticism will be making it possible for the same idea to be exposed to discussion. If the teen discovers for himself or herself the characteristics of the plan which make it unfeasible, he or she will abandon it much more willingly than if he or she was scorned and degraded for the proposal. Mutual respect is to be maintained at all times.

Nancy Gardner was a good student, the oldest of three children. She became interested in the study of medicine when she was a sophomore in high school and started to write to prestigious private universities with the idea of making application for premedical studies. When she spoke of her tentative plans to her parents, her mother was surprised at her daughter's determination to go far away from home, and her father was frightened at the high cost. They listened to her and thought about her proposals.

After Mr. and Mrs. Gardner spoke together about their concerns, they decided that they could not undertake the great expense of the kind of education Nancy wanted and proposed instead that she choose a school within a three hundred-mile radius of home that had the curriculum she wanted and the kind of student body into which she would fit comfortably.

Since the family had several years of practice in conducting a family council (see Chapter 6), Nancy and her parents were able to talk about her plans without hostility. She was disappointed and somewhat angry but recognized that she needed her parents' support, both emotionally and financially, and so she tried to find the way to maintain it. Because the search for a solution started before her junior year in high school, there was plenty of time to visit the campuses of several colleges and for Nancy to choose one within her parents' limitations. She eventually found one, applied, was accepted, and continued her studies.

Peter Wilson, aged fourteen, was bored with school and began to cut classes in his high school freshman year. His mother and father, both college graduates with advanced degrees, stressed the importance of education, but when Peter reached the legal age for dropping out, they signed their consent to his decision. They realized the futility of their own words at that time and saw that they could not force him to stay in school and learn. Peter got a job and worked to support himself until he realized that he wanted more job satisfaction than he was getting from his low-level job.

Peter's parents were very disappointed in his decision. They offered him his room and meals while he was out of school but no money of any kind. If he wanted anything beyond his room and board he had to earn the money for himself, which he did. He continued to be a welcome member of the family. From time to time he showed an interest in completing his high school education and occasionally took a course for that purpose. When he finished, he asked if he could have financial support to go on to college, but his parents required that he first demonstrate his determination to do so. They offered to pay half the cost of his first two terms in college. After several attempts he did complete the two terms, working part time to finance his share. Then, with the support of his parents, he enrolled full time in pursuit of the education he hopes will prepare him for a satisfying occupation.

The Wilsons were wise in requiring a proven commitment from Peter, since the decision to interrupt his education was his. By their requirement he had to take responsibility for himself and his decision. Had they not done so, they might have continued to spend money uselessly, resulting in their own resentment of their son's ingratitude. When parents resent the expenditures they make on behalf of their offspring, it is generally helpful to the relationship to stop spending the money and thereby quench the resentment.

Those two examples deal with higher education. But what about the young person who has no plans for college? Grace Hanson just wanted to get a job, to live at home, and spend her money. She wasn't interested in preparing for a career; she just wanted to earn and spend. Grace's parents decided that under those circumstances she would be required to pay for her room and board. They read classified advertisements and learned about the kind of housing arrangements that Grace could afford, then set a sum within the amount she would have to pay elsewhere. Grace had to decide whether living at home was worth her money. She chose to live elsewhere and thus learned to deal with the actual reality of supporting herself. She could not have had such an experience had her parents continued to provide shelter for her at no expense.

The Money Question

If money has been used before as a reward or as the price of specific achievements or behavior, its importance will be exaggerated and its amounts magnified when a child reaches adolescence. The wants become greater and the possibilities for rebellion are vastly expanded. The child who has been paid for doing household chores will expect greater pay in keeping with the greater expenses of teen activities. The child who has not been limited to an allowance but has always asked for money for school supplies, lunches, movies, and fun will ask for a car, ski trips, records, and the latest-fad clothing and hobbies. It is never too late, however, to decide on the limits and to adhere to them. There is danger in feeling sorry for a young person, for he or she is then likely to feel sorry for himself or herself, and in that state of mind one cannot function well.

Beware also of the thought, "I want my teen to have what I missed." The danger in this intention is that you the parent will expect to enjoy it through your child and you may be disappointed that tastes have changed. The adolescent who receives a car or a trip or a set of golf clubs because his or her parents never had them may not be enthusiastic about any of them and may prefer to forgo them if the price is everlasting gratitude. Neither do parents owe their children everything they crave, everything the neighbors have, or everything advertised.

The trouble with sacrificing for your children is that the children can never repay you, nor can you help wanting them to do so. Parents can set the time when they expect their youngsters to support themselves and set the limits on what they will pay for before then. There is no point in subsidizing them indefinitely; it only encourages young people to remain dependent.

The Other Questions

The other two tasks mentioned in the introduction are to establish heterosexual resolution and direction and integrate personality. These occur in the abstract, in thoughts and feelings. In the adolescent, work is going on all the time, whether or not it becomes evident. Personality becomes integrated as a gradual process that continues from earliest childhood, and it is probably never completely finished.

Choice of a partner has many visible effects and is one of the areas most fraught with danger of disagreement between parent and teen. With changes in society, young people feel free at an early age to engage in relationships and activities that were considered highly immoral even a decade ago. The choice of a companion will be made as a result of all the other aspects of personality and family relationships that have been discussed. Parents may or may not approve but cannot expect to control. As in other aspects of life, a power struggle will only prove who wins one battle. It does not enhance the quality of life. A parent may certainly express a personal opinion but may not expect that opinion to be shared. As in other decisions, it is most appropriate to listen to one another, to respect each other's viewpoints even in disagreement, and to remain friendly. Parents can be firm, meaning they respect themselves and their own views, but kind, meaning they respect their offspring's right to differ.

No matter how an adolescent decides to spend his or her future, the responsibility for the decision does not rest on the parents. Neither do parents own the credit for success or blame for failure. It is a mistake for parents to expect their children to fulfill their own ambitions, and it is also a mistake to take the glory when they do.

Each individual must live out his or her own life, recognize personal responsibility for how it develops, and accept the consequences of those decisions and actions. Even if the decisions of adolescence turn out to have been in error, there is always time to make new ones, to turn in new ways along new paths. Our culture now provides acceptance for new beginnings at any stage in life, and if a person has the continuing friendship of the people close to him or her, there is always opportunity for change and growth.

14
What Can a Parent Do?

Before you can hope to improve your personal relationships it is necessary to understand the theory behind a system of human interaction. Success does sometimes follow random changes in behavior, but it is more likely to occur if changes are made following a specific plan. The things we do ought to make sense in view of what we want to accomplish. But no amount of understanding theory and learning procedures can alone make the changes that lead to harmony between the generations.

A parent must act, and it is admittedly difficult to know how to begin. But there are steps you can follow. When you recognize conflict in your relationship, *stop* yourself before you say what seems to erupt or before you do what seems to be natural. Unless there is a grave emergency, it is usually helpful to postpone a decision or an action in order to:

• *Think about the purpose of your own feelings.* Are you trying to control your adolescent, to prove that you're smarter, to show that you can get your way?

• *Think about what you want to accomplish.* Do you want to achieve harmony? Are you willing to take steps that may be difficult? Are you willing to risk and to trust?

• *Act in new ways,* expressing the lessons you have learned in this book. Listen to, accept, and encourage your offspring.

• *Limit yourself to what you can do.* Mind your own business so that others can mind theirs.

Although you remove yourself from control and domination, stay connected in affection and mutual enjoyment of shared events and occupations.

This all sounds very general, and you may be disappointed at the lack of recipes for instant harmony, but solutions to family situations must fit the particular family, must be accessible to the family members, and must make sense according to expectable human behavior. The following story, which took place over twenty years ago, illustrates the development of a specific solution that is now widely recommended.

At that time Dr. Rudolf Dreikurs demonstrated his principles of family relationships before groups of parents, teachers, and counselors, most of whom were women. Very few fathers or male teachers were present. He taught that adults must learn to extricate themselves from the provocations of young children in order to break the pattern of the children's misbehavior. He showed that a child's excessive bids for attention would diminish when the target adult did not acknowledge them. He stressed that an adult must consider the situation in which the conflict occurred rather than the child's specific behavior and recommended that a mother leave the room or leave the house in order to demonstrate her independence from the child's demands.

In carrying out such a procedure, it is essential that the

adult be calm, and therefore one must depart quietly without anger and without warning. If the adult waits for anger, the opportunity for correction is lost. Many mothers reported how hard it was to walk out of the room, for they could still hear the children. Dr. Dreikurs suggested then that a mother who wanted to train her child and herself toward a better relationship should walk out of the house as soon as she began to feel the pressure of the child's demands.

Most of the mothers balked at that advice, especially in winter and especially if there were other younger children. As Dr. Dreikurs explained how essential it was for an adult actually to remove himself or herself from the child's presence, one of the mothers found the solution.

Mrs. McNeil discovered that she could extricate herself from her son's provocations by going into her bathroom and locking the door, staying there until the calling and whining stopped. She learned to recognize the initial signs of conflict and to leave before she got angry. Dr. Dreikurs was intrigued with her idea and further recommended that the bathroom be prepared beforehand as a place of refuge, with magazines to read, a transistor radio to be played at high volume, and a comfortable chair if possible.

This is not to suggest the bathroom technique as a solution to be used with your teen. It is much more likely that you can develop more suitable strategies. Since a teen has greater command of language than a young child, you need to learn to listen carefully.

In the spirit that you, the parent, can probably invent suitable solutions for the situations that trouble you, the examples that follow will set out specific incidents in which there was a conflict between parents and teenagers. Study each one individually, and before reading my comments, think about what you would do in such a situation. They are not presented as success stories but as material for consideration. My comments are intended to illuminate what is actually happening in each relationship and to suggest the direction parents need to take to work toward improvement.

Among your acquaintances are probably other parents of teens who are also troubled by the changes they see and experience. You can help each other if you join together to study these principles and discuss these examples. You will find you can be helpful to one another while you consider other people's problems. While the following examples may not describe your situation specifically, you may find areas of similarity that relate to your own family.

Miriam Schiff, Aged Fourteen

Miriam came home from school crying. She complained to her mother about Mrs. Forester, her home economics teacher, who was terribly unfair. Miriam had just received her report card and it showed "incomplete" in home economics. Miriam didn't think that was right. The project for the term was to sew a skirt, and she had done it. It was not incomplete. The difficulty arose because the skirt hemline wasn't even and Mrs. Forester insisted Miriam rip it out and resew it in class. The repair wasn't finished, nor even begun, on the last day of the grading period.

The rules of the class were that all work must be done in class; none can be brought home. Miriam wailed that if she had to redo her work during class time she would fall further behind and wouldn't ever catch up with the rest of her class. She thought the hemline was all right, that the teacher was mean, and that she should be allowed to go ahead with the next project. She cried to her mother and begged her to help.

Mrs. Schiff sent a polite note to Mrs. Forester. She said the skirt looked fine. She also said that if it didn't meet the standard, Miriam ought to get a low grade but not be further penalized. She suggested that if the skirt had to be repaired Miriam should be allowed to bring it home so that she wouldn't fall further behind with the other class work.

There was no response from Mrs. Forester. A few days later Mrs. Schiff telephoned the teacher at school. She repeated the suggestions she had written, maintaining a reasonable and courteous manner. Mrs. Forester did not agree. She insisted that the skirt be repaired during class time. Mrs. Schiff felt terrible. She had tried in every way to rescue her daughter and felt that she had failed to do so. Her sympathy for her daughter mingled with anger at the teacher. She couldn't understand her own ineffectiveness and felt defeated as a good mother.

When all her efforts proved futile and Miriam's tears subsided, Mrs. Schiff acknowledged to her daughter that she would have to follow Mrs. Forester's instructions. Miriam and her mother were both unhappy, but within two weeks Miriam had repaired the skirt hemline and caught up with her class on the next project. When she realized that her mother couldn't change the requirements of the classroom, she worked extra hard and met the standard eventually.

Question: How might Mrs. Schiff have acted in a different manner for Miriam's benefit?

COMMENT

Mrs. Schiff erred in trying to protect her daughter from her own responsibility for completing school work. Miriam is the second of three daughters. She follows a bright, competent sister who achieves well anything she wants to do. Mrs. Schiff realized after counseling that she was in the habit of shielding Miriam and that Miriam's adolescence was an opportunity to help her grow more independent. Rather than be shielded, Miriam needed to be encouraged to believe that she could meet life's challenges.

By intervening with the teacher, Mrs. Schiff communicated to Miriam a message that she wasn't competent to handle her schoolwork herself. She didn't need to say so; the fact that she was eager to take over, to "straighten it out," meant that she didn't believe Miriam could take care of it herself. Miriam begged her mother for help because she had always leaned on her for protection from difficulty. Her begging required a different response.

The better course would have been for Mrs. Schiff to listen carefully to Miriam's painful recital, to stay with her until the tears subsided, and then to say in an encouraging manner, "You'll be able to correct the hem and catch up with the class, too." Other words of encouragement that might be used are: "I guess you feel bad to have that 'incomplete' on your card, but as soon as you fix the skirt, you'll be able to get a grade." Or "Teachers do seem unfair sometimes, but usually the best way to cope is to follow instructions."

Because she had been shielded and protected as a young child, Miriam is now easily discouraged, and she needs encouragement in every possible way. Only by learning that she can cope with what appears to be a minor difficulty can she acquire the confidence to cope with what will certainly be greater problems in the future.

John Grant, Aged Nineteen

Mr. and Mrs. Grant counsulted me about John because they felt he didn't spend enough time at home with them. They had been giving him everything he wanted, including money for an expensive university, fraternity fees, air fare, clothes, etc., but in return they felt they were entitled to his companionship during vacations. Furthermore, they required him to work in his father's business during the long vacations and expected him to spend his salary as they directed.

The immediate conflict was whether or not John would come home on summer vacation the following year. John said he'd like to stay in the college town and work there. Mr. Grant was furious at this suggestion but began to doubt whether he could enforce his demands. The argument over next summer's plans was merely a symptom of a growing distance between him and his son. John had always conformed to his father's expectations, but as he got older he appeared to be less willing. Any time John didn't want to do what he was asked to do, Mr. Grant interpreted this response as disrespect. Furthermore, both Mr. and Mrs. Grant believed they had a right to expect a return on their money.

Subsequently, John came to see me alone. He told me he feared that he would lose his parents' love and their financial support if he didn't meet their demands and restrictions. He said he wanted to complete his education, but he didn't want to have to support himself in the meantime. He said he felt trapped; he couldn't figure out how to please both his parents and still become independent of them. John realized that this conflict was interfering with his studies, spoiling his social life, and hanging over him like an obsession all the time. He wanted his independence but did not want to defy his parents.

Question: What could John's parents do that might solve the conflicts between them and their son?

COMMENT

Mr. and Mrs. Grant erred in expecting John to pay them a return on their financial investment. Their demands on him were excessive and not only worked to create distance between John and themselves but to make a situation in which the financial bind was the most important one tying John to his parents. As soon as he would be able to support himself he would hold himself aloof from them.

Mr. and Mrs. Grant learned they could set limits on the amount of money they advanced to John and let him decide his own plans. The road to good relationships with one's offspring is not paved with money. When John discovered he couldn't always get "a few bucks more" his respect for his parents grew, and they learned that one of the greatest gifts they could give him was the opportunity to function independently—to make his own plans and to learn from his own mistakes.

Gail Jacobsen, Aged Fifteen

Gail asked for help in how to handle her boy friend. She felt as though he were beginning to monopolize her life and she felt unable to cope with the situation. When Gail first met Tom, she had found his attention flattering. It felt good to have a boy friend always available, ready with compliments and devotion. Even though she could see that he was confused about life and full of unsolved problems, she believed that she could help him. She observed his poor family life and considered it an excuse for his unusual behavior. She tried to compensate for his deficiencies.

But eventually, monopolizing all her free time, Tom tyrannized her and threatened suicide when she wanted to spend her time with her family or other friends. Gail, a good student, attractive and ambitious, felt trapped. It seemed to her that she was failing in this one aspect of her life in contrast to her many other successes.

The Jacobsens, Gail's parents, were aware of the pressure of the relationship and Tom's demands but were at a loss to help her. His threats of suicide frightened them as well as Gail. They didn't know how to help her break loose from Tom or how to convince her that it was not necessary for her to try to save him from unhappiness. They were arguing with Gail about what she should do, and the conflict infected the entire family.

Question: Could the Jacobsens help Gail?

COMMENT

In the relationship between Gail and Tom, there was very little that her parents could do. However, they could give Gail the emotional support and encouragement she needed while she learned a different way of perceiving herself. She needed to value her own life and well-being as well as Tom's and to realize that she could not make up to him for what he saw as deficits in his life, regardless of how much time and effort she devoted to him.

Gail, the oldest of three daughters, had found her place in the family by achievement and was accustomed to success in anything she undertook. In counseling, it was necessary to help her see her own overambition. Using an athletic metaphor, I told her she was trying to pole vault with the bar set at seven feet. I suggested to her that if she set it at two feet she could probably jump it easily and then work up to a higher level if she wished.

This enabled Gail to see how her personal goals were too high in many ways and she began to lower her demands on herself. Meanwhile, her parents learned to deemphasize honors and awards and stopped holding Gail up as a model of perfection to her younger sisters. Gradually Gail risked denying Tom's demands. His threats diminished when he saw they were ineffective, and Gail made new friends as the new school year began.

Dan Carlson, Aged Nineteen

Dan left school to go to work. He lived at home free and was often unemployed. With his father's help, he bought a car and then fell behind on the payments. He did not honor his commitments, but his parents felt sorry for him and continued to support him, give him money, and make his payments at the bank to shield him from harsh disapproval. They felt obliged to help him in this way because he had had a deprived childhood. Dan had been a sickly boy who was quickly overshadowed by the birth of a younger brother. His parents attributed his dependency to his earlier unhappiness.

One evening Dan brought his girl friend Sarah home and told his parents that they needed a small favor, just a signature. Since Sarah had a good job, Dan said he and she had decided that they would take an apartment together.

They already had found a nice place at a modest cost and needed only his father's signature on a lease before they could move in. Dan and Sarah were certain that Mr. Carlson would sign because they fully intended to keep up the rent and the Carlsons would have no obligation.

Stunned, Dan's parents asked for time to think it over. Their moral and religious scruples restrained them from endorsing such an arrangement, but they did not wish to deny Dan anything that would make him happy. Mr. and Mrs. Carlson came for counseling in order to help them reach a decision.

Question: What should the Carlsons have done?

COMMENT

By their previous actions, the Carlsons had given Dan the impression that he could have anything he wanted from them. They were trying to be generous, but the family income was not large, and meeting Dan's payments often had meant falling behind in other obligations. Meanwhile, they resented the continual drain on their resources.

In counseling, they decided that they would no longer perpetuate Dan's dependency but would refuse to cooperate in helping him undertake further financial obligations. They did not remind him of his past failures—there had been enough arguments and recriminations before—but Mr. Carlson refused to sign the lease. He told his son that he would like to see him develop his own good credit rating and would always be available to discuss future plans.

The Carlsons' refusal removed their resentment, for they felt relieved of the burden of paying for Dan's wants. By ceasing to indulge him they stopped feeling sorry for him and their mutual respect grew when Dan, faced with meeting his own obligations, devoted more effort to his work and developed a more consistent employment record.

In this situation, the parents needed to reassess their responsibilities and to decide on limits. When they did, their son was disappointed, but the long-range relationship improved. Gradually Dan began to feel more confident and competent in managing his own affairs.

Laura Gilbert, Aged Thirteen

Laura belonged to a social group of ten girls who met weekly at the local community center. The distance from home was too far to walk, so parents of the girls had agreed to take turns driving them there and bringing them home.

Mrs. Gilbert, a conscientious parent, disapproved when she discovered that sometimes the driver who appeared to take Laura was not a parent but a teen-aged brother or sister of one of Laura's friends. She refused to let Laura ride in a car driven by an adolescent and told her that any time a teen driver came she would take Laura to the center herself.

Laura, the youngest girl in the group, was sensitive over the teasing she often received from the others about being treated like a baby. She didn't want to be treated differently from anyone else in the group.

Mrs. Gilbert suggested that she would telephone the other parents to complain about the chauffeuring arrangements, but Laura was afraid that that too would make her look childish in the eyes of her friends. Laura just wanted to continue to ride with the other girls no matter who was driving. Defiantly, she told her mother that she could always lie to her about it to prevent her mother from knowing who actually drove the car.

Question: Could Mrs. Gilbert achieve her purpose?

COMMENT

Initially, Mrs. Gilbert saw only two choices: to turn Laura loose to danger, or to take her to the center alone each week. She could not consider the first, and if she insisted on the second, she would prolong the conflict that had begun between her and her daughter. Riding with her mother, Laura would miss the companionship of the other girls en route. She would feel singled out for protection and feel she had to defend the other parents, who, in Mrs. Gilbert's eyes, were at fault for not keeping their word.

Another angle to the conflict showed itself when Laura threatened to lie. Mrs. Gilbert did not want her daughter to lie. She had always been truthful, in accordance with her family's values.

Mrs. Gilbert had to reconsider her own priorities. Telling the truth was first. Second was the value for her daughter of the supervised experience at the community center. Third was safety in an automobile. She realized that she could not absolutely guarantee her daughter's safety, since accidents happen when adults are driving too. Instead of calling the other parents, she became better acquainted with the older teens who were driving and reassured herself that they were responsible people.

Through trusting the other drivers, Mrs. Gilbert showed her trust in Laura, who began to move away from the protection of her parents into the wider world.

Neddie Renfrew, Aged Seventeen

Neddie and his parents were referred for family counseling by the juvenile officer in the local court. He was under suspicion of burglary after being apprehended trying to break into a motel room. The juvenile officer believed that the family situation of which Neddie was a part contributed to his delinquent behavior and instructed the Renfrews to learn better ways of dealing with their son.

Neddie was assertive about his behavior. He said straightforwardly that he could do whatever he wanted when his father was drinking, because "Mom can't lay a hand on me." He said he purposely timed his escapades to take place while his father was on a drinking binge. Ned Renfrew, the father, held a job sometimes but was often out of work because of his drinking habits. Mrs. Renfrew carried the major financial responsibility for the family. She worked full time at a job through which she was often able to secure employment for other family members, including Neddie. She ran the household, made the decisions, and took care of everybody.

Despite his father's behavior and his mother's dominance, Neddie perceived his father as the all-powerful "real man" and didn't feel he could ever live up to his father's standards. Ned Renfrew, trying to impress his son, would run up massive debts buying motorcycles, cars, and other things for Neddie. He believed that it would really make Neddie behave if he bought the things he asked for. Mr. Renfrew was deep in debt for vehicles he bought that Neddie had wrecked beyond repair.

Although there was a younger son, a "good" boy, the parents were unwilling to examine the relationships among all the family members. They persisted in asking for the key to Neddie's behavior, saying repeatedly, "We'll do anything to help him."

Question: How can Neddie be helped?

COMMENT

The Renfrews had to stop buying things for Neddie so that he would feel responsible for his own needs. Mr. Renfrew would have to stay sober. Mrs. Renfrew would have to stop "taking care" of everybody. She had been in the habit of excusing her husband when he was too drunk to go to work and of carrying the burden of the bills her husband incurred.

To begin Neddie's rehabilitation, both parents would have to treat him and each other with respect, as equals sharing responsibilities. When they terminated counseling, they said they understood how the family relationships had affected Neddie as well as others and they they had begun to make the necessary changes.

Neddie never had to endure the consequences of his own behavior. He may discover that he cannot always avoid the requirements of the law, or he may choose to direct his efforts toward getting and keeping a job and taking on responsibility for his own well-being.

There was no simple practical solution for Neddie. There might have been prevention.

Ursula Norton, Aged Eighteen

When Ursula's eighteenth birthday came, she was a senior in high school. She complained that the midnight curfew she agreed to when she was a sixteen-year-old sophomore was now too early. For those two years she had willingly come in at midnight on weekends and asked for extra privileges on special occasions.

Her father reported the family conflict and how it was solved:

After her eighteenth birthday she began coming in a half hour to an hour late. I screamed at her and her date but made no impression. One night it was 2:00 A.M. and we had a loud yelling fight about it. She refused to give in and claimed that she was old enough to handle that part of her life and that we had no right to impose a curfew on her.

I said that as long as she ate my food and lived in my house I would make the rules. I wanted to settle it right there, but my wife persuaded me to stop the argument, go to sleep, and finish the discussion the next morning when we were all more calm. While I was fighting with Ursula my wife stayed out if it. She had been studying and thinking about what we should do. She convinced me that Ursula was trustworthy and dependable and that the curfew was becoming the cause of too much disruption in the household. Since there was no longer any valid reason to maintain a curfew, we ought to remove it. When we told her so in the morning, Ursula was amazed.

For the next three weekends she stayed out until at least 4:00 A.M. and once until 6:00 A.M. We held our tongues. On Friday night of the fourth weekend she came in at 10:30 P.M., and I asked if she felt all right, because it was so early.

She replied, "Daddy, it's no fun staying out all night just for the heck of it. Besides, I'm really tired."

Question: What issues were involved in the conflict between father and daughter?

The curfew was not the issue. The issue was who would win the tug-of-war. Mr. Norton wanted to show that he was provider and therefore boss, and Ursula wanted to prove she could be independent. The curfew had been unchanged for two years during which time Ursula had grown closer to adulthood.

In the tug-of-war, as long as Mr. Norton held on to his end and pulled mightily, Ursula pulled in the other direction. When he let go and showed that he would trust his daughter, she found there was no fun in rebellion if there was nobody to rebel against. He paved the way for friendship and communication by treating her with respect and giving her credit for good judgment.

Tim Roberts, Aged Sixteen

Tim cried often. Mr. and Mrs. Roberts had asked his pediatrician when he would outgrow the crying spells. They were beginning to wonder if he ever would. He did very little school work, spent most of his time after school all alone, and wouldn't fight back if anybody attacked him. Judo lessons didn't help, because Tim liked to be thrown but wouldn't throw anyone else.

Mr. Roberts was most concerned. Tim was his only son; there were two younger sisters who caused no problems. Mrs. Roberts cried easily too, and both parents feared their son wouldn't be able to get along in the world if he continued to be timid and weepy.

They reported that although Tim had friends, he wouldn't go anywhere with them even when they did occasionally call for him. At school he attempted to get on the basketball team, but he wasn't aggressive on the court. He tried for a part in a dramatic production but didn't try for the leading role. It became apparent that Mr. Roberts expected his son to excel in everything and felt personally injured by Tim's passivity and tears.

Tim wore the attitude of an injured soul. He said he should be able to do only what he wanted only when he wanted. He complained about pressure from his mother to do well in school and yet acknowledged that he didn't do much work. He said he could never make up his mind which subject to work on first, so he couldn't accomplish anything. He said his grades were never as good as his parents expected, and when they told him to work harder he would try but just couldn't keep it up.

Question: Can Tim's parents stop his crying?

COMMENT

The purpose of Tim's weeping was to keep both his parents in his service. When he began to cry, both parents felt helpless and immediately ceased their demands on him and tried to be kind. Tim didn't believe he could make his way in life by being competent, especially since his sister, only two years younger, had proved she could excel in anyting she attempted.

Tim said, "When you're in a battle with another person, the one who gives up wins." His device for putting this into practice was to turn on the "water power"—the tears.

Improvement came when the Robertses began to stay out of the squabbles between Tim and his sister Helen. In this way they demonstrated that they could trust Tim to handle a quarrel. Without their intervention, there was no audience for the tears, nor did Helen have to show her power.

The Robertses also discontinued their pressure and their inquiries about Tim's schoolwork, and he later said, "With the pressure off, school is a breeze." His grades proved it.

By succumbing to Tim's attitude of helplessness and by holding excessively high standards, the Robertses had helped to perpetuate their son's feelings of inadequacy. When they began instead to demonstrate confidence in him, he was able to have confidence in himself and to enjoy the company of his sister rather than to see her as his rival. The tears stopped because they lost their purpose.

Pam Sutton, Aged Fifteen

Pam's mother brought her for counseling after Pam was apprehended by a police officer at 6:00 A.M. She was with a boy friend in his parked car. She received a curfew warning ticket requiring that her parent or guardian come with her to the police station the following day. Mrs. Sutton was furious, regarding this as proof of Pam's delinquency. She wanted to have Pam "straightened out."

Pam was the second of three daughters. Her parents had been divorced when she was twelve after years of dissension punctuated by temporary separations. Mrs. Sutton was working full time, struggling to support her daughters and herself and to manage the household. Pam had been her mother's darling until she was six, when her sister Kitty was born. At that time she felt dethroned and deprived when she saw her mother paying attention to the baby. It was then that she first intensified her infantile ways of getting attention and service.

By the time Pam entered her teens, Mrs. Sutton had lost patience with her, often telling her that she was a carbon copy of her father and therefore no good. She said she had been glad to get rid of him. Pam commented, "It's not my fault he was my father. She could have picked better."

Pam's school history was poor. She attended a parochial school through eighth grade. At that school she felt she was being watched every minute, and although she didn't like it, she complied with the rules. She said that when she reached the public high school it seemed that nobody cared whether or not she came to school or attended class. She was expelled from the freshman class for repeated absences and transferred to a different special school, which she refused to attend. She excused her truancy on the grounds that she should not be expected to go to school with strangers.

At home, Pam contrived to get much service from other family members, beginning in the early morning when she refused to be awakened. She claimed to be a very sound sleeper. Mrs. Sutton and Marie, the older sister, were kept busy each day trying to rouse Pam. Although household jobs were divided among the four family members, Pam refused to do any work, so Marie did her jobs for her, knowing that Mrs. Sutton would be enraged if she came home from work to find dirty dishes in the sink.

Pam didn't see why she should do any work at home, since it seemed to her that she was excluded from the family circle. She said she wanted to go to school but felt lost and alone without friends and didn't believe she could make friends. She said she felt she was getting nowhere and had no confidence that she could change anything about her life. Her feelings of defiance alternated with feelings of complete discouragement. In Pam's view, the only way to get anyone to notice her or care about her was to break the rules. She felt as if she were all alone in enemy territory, constantly under the danger of attack from unfriendly forces.

Question: What was Pam's main purpose in staying out until 6:00 A.M.?

COMMENT

The purpose of staying out all night was to defy Mrs. Sutton and to test her ability to control Pam. Of course, Pam was probably enjoying herself, too, and was not aware that this was only one more battle in her rebellion. Although Pam did not actively seek to be arrested, she knew that she risked additional conflict at home.

Pam began to give up rebellion when her mother ceased to harass her for one week. In counseling, Mrs. Sutton agreed to make no demands for the week and give no service. During that week Pam attended school, did her assignments, and made progress toward catching up with her classes. Her sullen mien occasionally broke into a smile, and there were other signs that she believed others cared about her.

With this development, Mrs. Sutton reluctantly began to believe that Pam could be a valued member of the family. When Marie stopped doing Pam's chores, Pam did most of them. They had a family council meeting in which the jobs were shifted so that no one bore an unfair load, and Mrs. Sutton discovered that she did not have to assign the jobs but that together they could all allot them. No one reminded Pam to get up in the morning, and she discovered that she could really hear the alarm when it rang.

Pam's rebellion did not cease suddenly and completely,

but each small step that she took toward being responsible helped to convince her mother and sisters that she could be trusted. The atmosphere in the family improved gradually. First Marie and Pam found they could be friends, then Pam and Kitty. As this developed, Pam began to feel that she really belonged in her own family and decided she could make new friends in school as well.

Jerry Vonack, Aged Fourteen

Jerry was a freshman in high school but attended rarely. He cut classes so often that when he did occasionally attend he couldn't understand the subject matter. In addition, he stayed out late with friends and smoked heavily. His father and mother had imposed "grounding," requiring him to be home at 3:30 P.M. and stay home, sometimes for weeks on end, but Jerry disregarded their instructions. At times he would conform to being grounded, but as soon as the period of punishment was finished, he would again wander after school hours. His behavior convinced his father that he was "no good," and his mother became obsessed with worry about his future.

Jerry had been tested earlier and found to have above-average intelligence and very little self-confidence. He was the younger of two, with a sister four years older, a college freshman. She was an excellent student and consistently had made the high school honor roll. Her parents' main concern with her was that she set such high standards for herself. She and Jerry would often fight when they were both at home together.

In addition to their worry about Jerry's absences from school, Mr. and Mrs. Vonack were concerned about money missing from Mr. Vonack's drawer. A neighbor for whom Jerry often babysat also complained that money was missing after Jerry had been there. When the Vonacks asked him about the money he became sullen and silent.

Question: How can the Vonacks make sure Jerry goes to class?

COMMENT

The Vonacks could not guarantee that Jerry would go to class or if he did that he would learn, but they found they could change their relationships in such a way that it became more likely that he would. Jerry discovered very early in life that he couldn't be first best, and so he chose to be first worst. The standards for scholastic achievement in his family were very high, and he didn't believe he could compete with his sister in reaching them.

By the time he enrolled in high school, Jerry was thoroughly discouraged and didn't believe he could do ordinary schoolwork. He managed to keep his parents preoccupied with him by behaving contrary to their directives. When his sister left for college, Jerry felt that he was constantly under a magnifying glass, receiving his parents' entire attention as they tried to make him successful according to their plans.

Jerry confided in counseling that he would like to please his parents, but since he had decided he could not, he wanted to get revenge against them. His parents were present when he said this and were shocked to hear it, for they truly believed all the time that they were acting in his best interests.

The only way Jerry's parents could help him was to allow him to be the master of his own life and to treat him with respect rather than with pressure. They had already discovered that punishment didn't work. It was evident that Jerry was doing only what he wanted, and their task was to stop protecting him from the consequences.

When Mr. Vonack realized that his scornful comments to his son discouraged him and stimulated him to further rebellion rather than to conformity with his father's wishes, and Mrs. Vonack realized that her protective ways were not appropriate for an adolescent, they began to trust Jerry to want to make the most of his own life. They were able to help him to enroll in an alternate high school program that allowed him to do his schoolwork in a freer atmosphere than the regular classroom.

All four family members have been and still are learning to cooperate with one another, to respect and trust one another, and to listen attentively. The lectures Mr. Vonack enjoyed giving ceased, and Mrs. Vonack stopped checking up on Jerry. He and his sister get along better together when she's at home, and he's attending school regularly and keeping up with his work.

Only when he felt he was being treated like a responsible person could Jerry act like one.

Afterword

Now that you've come this far with me, I hope that you do not feel overwhelmed by all the things I've told you to do. Consider that you already have had many good influences on your children. Remember those accomplishments and don't berate yourself for the mistakes you may have made. Sometimes what seems to have been a mistake turns out to have been a valuable decision. We cannot predict the future, and we don't always have a way of testing whether a decision was right. If you develop the courage to be imperfect, you can continue to act in new ways, and some of them will bring promising results.

The most gratifying result of parenthood, I believe, is a lifetime of friendship with the younger generation. Such a goal is of higher value than any other reward.

This book is directed to the average family struggling with the expected disruptions of adolescence. Its thrust is to help parents learn to improve the relationship between themselves and their teenagers. I haven't attempted to deal with the problems of exaggerated behavior: lawbreaking, drug taking, or sexual interactions. If such activity brings problems to your family, seek the assistance of a qualified family counselor as soon as you can. To find a qualified person, begin with the counseling staff of your local high school or consult your pediatrician or clergyman. Try to make sure that the person you consult is well trained and accredited; don't be afraid to ask him or her about qualifications. Read selectively and study the available material written for parents. The bibliography that follows will help you find ideas to expand your knowledge. It is not a confession of weakness to seek help; it is, rather, an acknowledgment of human imperfection, a trait we all share.

As I began this book by describing my first maternal experiences, I will close by telling you about a recent incident that involved my youngest son, Chuck, aged nineteen. It proved conclusively the value of the principles set forth in the preceding chapters. I have tremendous satisfaction knowing that trust, mutual respect, and recognizing parental limitations can be so powerful in maintaining warm relationships between parents and adolescent.

Chuck was at home on vacation between college terms. Five days each week he went to work, then had two full days off. Recently, he planned to visit friends on campus during his free time. Since this required a three-hour drive, he prepared to leave in the evening after work and thus have two full days to play.

When he was ready to leave home on Sunday night, it was raining very heavily, hail had begun to fall, and a tornado had just touched down in the area through which he would drive. It seemed foolhardy to go out into the storm. My husband suggested he wait until the rain eased up. Chuck grumbled, fidgeted, walked around the house a while, and then announced that he was leaving. The storm had not abated. He said, "Goodbye. I'll call you when I get there and I'll be back Tuesday night." Although he knew he left against our wishes, his respect for us showed in his promise to call on arrival.

We were extremely uneasy, but we did not want to create a vocal storm inside. We were worried about Chuck's safety and about the car, which was over five years old with mechanical problems. To us it seemed he was courting danger, but it was clear that he was determined to leave, and he's too big and strong to be detained by physical force.

We retired to try to sleep. Four hours later, we discussed whether to call the state police or the highway department to try to find out what had happened to Chuck. The radio news reported hundreds of cars stalled in the expressway on which he would travel, traffic tied up for miles, and extensive storm damage in the tornado area. Nearly five hours after he left, he returned, telling us he had been stalled in the flooded expressway twenty miles from home. It took him four hours to leave the expressway and find a way to get back home.

Of course we were tremendously relieved and did not scold him or remind him of our earlier cautionary remarks. We merely told him emphatically how glad we were that he returned home safely. Our relief was intensified by additional news reports of serious injury to persons similarly trapped by the storm.

In the morning before Chuck resumed his trip he told me he knew that it was stupid to leave in the storm, but his wish to arrive before daylight and see his friends was stronger than his intellectual knowledge that he was risking danger. He said he trusted himself as a driver, even in the heavy rain, and was worried only about whether the car would withstand the strain. As he talked, I thought about what his mood might have been had we had a big fight before he left.

Anger wouldn't help him be careful, nor would it have allowed him to turn around and return home. Were there anger and hostility between us, his defiance could have moved him onward in an attempt to prove that he was right.

When he left the second time, he drove away in bright sunshine, leaving behind a cheerful goodbye. Three hours later he telephoned to report his safe arrival.

We learned from that event, and I hope you will too. We might have argued with Chuck and tried to persuade him that it was ridiculous to undertake a trip under those weather conditions. We might have reminded him that he is young and inexperienced, which is true, and that we have had much more experience, which is also true. The argument could have expanded to a major confrontation.

When we talked about it in the morning, Chuck said, "I wouldn't have argued. I would just have been furious and left sooner."

Even if we had been successful in persuading him to wait until morning, he would have resented our interference in his life. Either way there would have been hostility between us, with the possible addition of conflict between my husband and me if one of us had shared Chuck's viewpoint and "taken sides."

By realizing our own limitations and not trying to stop him, we allowed him to experience the consequences of an action that he knew was stupid. He surely has learned a lesson he will never forget. All of us have a memory now that will unite us when we recall it instead of one that will summon unpleasant feelings.

When we allow our teens to make their own decisions, we give them the opportunity to learn, to shift their course of action, to change their minds. There is no loss of face for either parents or offspring. But when we make decisions for them, we invite resentment and we assume the responsibility that should be theirs.

The qualities required for a harmonious relationship with teens work well in all human relationships: trust, mutual respect, honesty, minding one's own business. The corresponding movements are to listen, to encourage, and to accept.

The parents who develop relationships that include those attributes will not only help their sons and daughters to reach the full extent of their capabilities but will themselves find the freedom to be individuals, to grow in the realization of fuller, freer, more satisfying lives.

It's worth the effort.

Suggested Reading

Adler, Alfred. *The Science of Living.* Garden City, N.Y.: Doubleday Anchor Books, 1969.

———. *What Life Should Mean to You.* New York: G. P. Putnam's Sons, 1958.

Allred, G. Hugh. *On the Level.* Provo, Utah: Brigham Young University Press, 1974.

Anderson, Wayne J. *How to Discuss Sex with Teen-agers.* Minneapolis: T. S. Denison & Co., 1969.

Beecher, William, and Beecher, Marguerite. *Beyond Success and Failure.* New York: Julian Press, 1966.

Brodsky, Paul. *Adolescence.* New York: Libra Publishers, 1966.

———. "Problems of Adolescence: An Adlerian View," in *Adolescence* 3 (1968): 9–22.

DeRosis, Helen. *Parent Power/Child Power.* Indianapolis: Bobbs-Merrill, 1974.

Dinkmeyer, Don, and McKay, Gary. *Raising a Responsible Child.* New York: Simon and Schuster, 1973.

Dreikurs, Rudolf. *Adult-child Relations: A Workshop on Group Discussion with Adolescents.* Eugene, Ore.: Oregon University Press, 1961.

_____. *Children: The Challenge.* New York: Hawthorn Books, 1964.

_____, and Grey, Loren. *A Parents' Guide to Child Discipline.* New York: Hawthorn Books, 1970.

_____, Gould, Shirley, and Corsini, Raymond J. *Family Council.* Chicago: Henry Regnery, 1974.

Ellis, Alfred. "Talking to Adolescents about Sex," in *Rational Living* 2 (1967): 7–12.

Lombardi, Donald. *Search for Significance.* Chicago: Nelson-Hall, 1975.

Messer, Mitchell. *Handy Guide for Remaining Unpregnant.* Chicago: Illegitimacy Prevention Service, 1976.

Nikelly, A. D. "The Dependent Adolescent," in *Adolescence* 6 (1971): 139–144.

Reich, Luna. "An Adolescent's Behavior Problem," in K. A. Adler and Danica Deutsch, eds., *Essays in Individual Psychology.* New York: Grove Press, 1959.

Satir, Virginia. *Peoplemaking.* Palo Alto: Science and Behavior Books, 1972.

Southard, Helen F. *Sex before Twenty.* New York: E. P. Dutton, 1967.

Index

Index

Index